Macdonald was late for Dinner

❖

A Slice of Culinary Life in Early Canada

Macdonald was late for Dinner

❖

A Slice of Culinary Life in Early Canada

Patricia Beeson

broadview press
1993

For my great friend and endlessly enduring husband, John,
and for Richard, James, Nicholas, Kathryn and Alexander.

Canadian Cataloguing in Publication Data

Beeson, Patricia, 1932-   .
Macdonald was late for dinner: a slice of culinary life in early Canada.

Includes index.
ISBN 15511-022-9
1. Cookery, Canadian. I. Title
TX715. 6. B44 1993   641.5971   C93-094687-1

Broadview Press
Post Office Box 1243, Peterborough, Ontario, Canada. K9J 7H5

in the United Sates of America:
Post Office Box 670, Lewiston, New York 14092, USA

in the United Kingdom:
c/o Drake Marketing Services, Saint Fagan's Road, Fairwater, Cardiff, UK, CF53AE.

Broadview Press gratefully acknowledges the support of the Canada Council, the Ontario Arts Council, and the Ontario
Publishing Centre.

Cover design by George Kirkpatrick, photograph by Wayne Eardly.

Printed in Canada

1 2 3 4 5 6 7 8 9 10 11

Contents

Introduction

This is not a gourmet cook's cookbook. Rather, it is a collection of old recipes found in different areas around Ontario with some related local history, of an anecdotal but historically accurate kind. The book can be enjoyed by cooks as well as non-cooks. The stories and recipes mainly date from the time of the province's earliest settlement, although a few were produced in the 1920s and 30s. The copious illustrations of scenes and people which complement the material, are old photographs, not paintings, to emphasize the reality of the subject matter.

At the same time, while concentrating on Ontario material, I selected, where possible and feasible, whatever would connect the province with the wider world. For instance, although readers outside the province might never have heard of Thunder Bay, they certainly have heard of Arthur Conan Doyle; and where Temagami might not be familiar, Grey Owl is. Leaskdale is little known, even in Ontario, but certainly all Canadians and many others, have heard of Lucy Maude Montgomery, whose old housekeeper gave me two L.M.M. recipes and some intriguing insights into her family life. One Ottawa cookbook lent me was used in the Rideau Hall circles of the Minto era and has connections with Sir John A. Macdonald, first Prime Minister of Canada.

Although not Canada's biggest province, Ontario is still enormous. Total the areas of France, Germany, Greece and Belgium, and Ontario still has a little space to spare. Texas would fit easily into its "empty" northern half — but we don't boast about such things! Collecting this material took me all over the province, even north in a tiny plane from Thunder Bay to a remote Indian village, Lansdowne House, between the Manitoba border and James Bay. There I learned authentic northern Ojibway ways of preparing food. Other recipes were found in libraries, special collections, archives, and museums; many private individuals passed along the recipes, books, or oral traditions of their parents, grandparents, and earlier forebears. Too little has been made of the long existence of many ethnic groups in the province, so I have made a special point of focusing on the traditional food and background of a number of them. Some are very familiar, like the Indians or French-Canadians, but some have so low a profile outside their own area that the average Ontarian is barely aware of their existence. Among these are the Finns, especially around Thunder Bay; the Kashoubs south of Algonquin Park; the blacks in south-west Ontario; and a group of Mennonites who have lived for nearly 200 years in Markham, outside the main body in the Kitchener-Waterloo area.

Because of the range and variety of heritages in Toronto, that city contributes a large amount of material. Other fascinating places, groups and characters, it will be complained, are not mentioned at all and I am only too aware of it. Deciding what to include was a torment but everything could not go in. In some cases, a place is not included because I simply failed to unearth old recipes in the limited time I could spend to search. Perhaps some day there may be another book to remedy this.

As an additional wrinkle, in areas famed for a specific product (either now or in the past only) I hunted for old local recipes using that product. You will find recipes for apples in Thornbury, cheese in Ingersoll, and whitefish in Sault Ste. Marie.

I applied the criteria that the recipes, handwritten, oral or printed, must have been either produced in Ontario, or if from elsewhere, used in the province for a meaningful period of time. Furthermore, in order to experience the different factors affecting early cooks and cooking I took two courses in the old kitchens at Fort York.

The local historic aspect is of great importance to the book. Endeavouring to ensure accuracy I read quantities of local history, biography and autobiography; unearthing relevant old photographs was a special delight.

My hope is that not just cooks and historians, but visitors to Ontario, the residents of the towns and cities mentioned, in fact any person with a love for, or even just a passing interest in, this province, may read the book and find it interesting, authoritative, and, most importantly of all, enjoyable.

It was difficult to arrive at a consistent approach to the recipes I have gathered together. I have marked with a star those tested. This emphatically does not mean that they are preferable, only that I can pass an informed opinion on them. Most were good, some excellent. But what does one do with a few that are dull or inaccurate? However, because they tell us something about the people behind them and the times and the circumstances (how little, for instance, pioneers like Catherine Parr Traill had to be content with) I decided that, like history, these recipes didn't necessarily have to have happy outcomes and, apart from minimal corrections, just had to be accepted, warts and all. Perhaps with a warning hint!

Many recipes had very inadequate instructions and several none at all. This wasn't unusual as professional cooks knew on reading the ingredients what to do with them. In those cases I had the temerity to offer my own instructions. Also, old recipes were often for huge amounts, to feed large families, economise on fuel and effort, or use up a windfall, or all these, so I tended to reduce huge amounts in those tested.

The following abbreviations are used throughout the book:

t= teaspoon, T= tablespoon, c= cup.

I have organised the material as if pursuing a journey, with sidetrips, around the province, which is shaped somewhat like a huge, misshapen, largely landlocked Italy. We start at the 'toe' — Amherstburg in the southwest — and follow a path along the sole of the 'foot'. Then we turn north to Ottawa, and from there head into the north and west.

Acknowledgements

I am very grateful indeed for the help of a great many people whose efforts often went far beyond the bounds of ordinary obligation.

Among them are, most especially: Fiona Lucas, senior domestic interpreter at Fort York, Toronto, for information and help; Christine Niarchos-Bourolias, and the staff at the Archives of Ontario; the staff at the Baldwin Room, Metro Toronto Public Library; the staff at the Toronto Archives, City Hall; Juanita Farrell of Christie, Brown and Co, Nabisco Brands; and Leo O'Flaherty of the Department of Indian Affairs. I would also like to thank Mrs. Stanislava Marcovic of the Serbian Heritage Museum, Windsor; Dennis Carter-Edwards of Environment Canada Parks Service, Cornwall; and Bob Garcia, of Fort Malden Historic Site, Canadian Parks Service, for much help and suggesting new avenues; Betty Simpson of the North American Black Historical Museum for taking me in out of season; Kathryn Schwenger of the Chatham-Kent Museum; Alice Newby of the Raleigh Township Museum; Deborah Herkimer of the Elgin County Museum, St.Thomas; Shirley Lovell of the Ingersoll Cheese Museum; Bill Nesbitt of Dundurn Castle, Hamilton; Bill Severin of the Niagara Historical Society and Museum in Niagara-on-the-Lake, and, especially, researcher Joy Ormsby.

I also thank Allan McGillivray, at the Uxbridge-Scott Museum; the tireless Peggy Hohenadel at the Wingham Museum; Susan Bassett and Lynne Campbell at the Ontario Agricultural Museum; Judy McGonigal of the Sault Ste.Marie Museum; Maria Santi, of the Sudbury Multicultural Folklore Association for wonderful introductions; Nada Nehes, at the Sudbury Civic Square Library; Jack Schecter, Librarian at Upper Canada Village; Jean McNiven, Librarian and heroic researcher at the Bytown Museum, Ottawa ; Jane Foster of the Lennox and Addington County Museum, Napanee; Donna Dumbledon, Douglas Collection, Queen's University, Kingston; Suzanne Knight, Markham Museum; Thorold Tronrud, at the Thunder Bay Museum for well-researched answers to endless questions; Lois Heald at the Paipoonge Museum, outside Thunder Bay; and Marianne Mackenzie of the Peterborough Centennial Museum and Archives.

I would like to mention with gratitude the following private individuals for their help with information, assistance, and often the loan of material: in Toronto, Maury Reddon, Julie Deeks, Robin Harmer, Sandra Temes; Lorna Humphries, Mary Stoklosa, Diana Salmond, Lucienne Watt, and most particularly, the late Gilbert Powell Sladen; Kate Clendenning, historian, Blenheim; Shannon Prince in Merlin; the Reverend Peg Wheeler of St.Peter's Church, Tyrconnel, for going right out of her way; Illean Popov, Windsor; Dorothy Reesor, Markham; Jane Snider, Ocean Springs, MS, USA; Elsie Davidson in Uxbridge; Jack Mitchell in Thornbury; Mary Armstrong in Clarksburg; Gwen Robinson, Chatham; Tina Florio in Burlington; Martin Shulist, Wilno; Madeline Theriault in North Bay; Lucille Mackenzie, Temagami; Betty Wilson, in Peterborough; Anniki Maki and Margot Lebelle in Sudbury; Kerine Budner in Thunder Bay; Cecilia Sugarhead, Lansdowne House; and especially James Westhaver, school principal, Lansdowne House, who most generously lent me his accomodation in his absence.

A Battalion (12th York Rangers) in formation known as the "British Square," 1860s.

The Soldier's Wife

In the extreme southwest of Ontario lies Amherstburg, edging the reedy banks of the Detroit River, which is all that prevents the long toe of the province's malformed foot from prodding indelicately into Michigan's eastern flank. Like many early Ontario border towns it was important strategically for guarding the frontier against American attack. With this in view, the British fortified it in 1796. The site, now known as Fort Malden, was captured and briefly held by the Americans during the War of 1812. Later, in the Rebellion of 1837, supporters of William Lyon Mackenzie were repelled when they attacked the fort, while those manning the schooner "Anne," which had bombarded the town, were captured when it ran aground. Five years later, a company of the Royal Canadian Rifle Regiment was stationed in the fort. Among their number was Ensign William Kingsmill, born on St. Helena when his father, also a soldier, was posted there during Napoleon's imprisonment on the island. It wasn't long before Ensign Kingsmill met and married Louisa Innis. Louisa, who appears to have been a capable young woman, kept herself busy about her home, which was one of the earliest built in Amherstburg, on the corner of Dalhousie and Gore Streets. In 1845, the year her husband was promoted to Lieutenant and posted south of Montreal, she filled the pages of an account book with her beautifully written "Receipt Book." The account book, bought in Montreal, suggests she may have accompanied her husband to this posting.

Several of the recipes were obviously provided by other officer's wives, and on occasion, by the officers themselves. No doubt food, along with the latest news of postings and more intimate regimental gossip, was an essential element of the wives' conversation. A Mrs. Cox contributed the recipe below. Married into the 34th Regiment which had been stationed at Amherstburg in 1838 and 1839, she may have been Louisa's sister.

34TH REGIMENT'S COLD PUNCH*

[This is a very enjoyable lemony drink, but deceptively powerful. The quantity will serve 50-60 people]

Take 24 lemons, peel them and steep the rinds in 2 qts. of rum for 12 hours. Add 2 qts. brandy, the juice of two doz. lemons, 3 ½ lbs. loaf sugar, 6 qts. cold water and 2 qts. boiling new milk. Stir well till the milk curdles. Let it stand 3 hrs. closely covered and strain through a flannel jelly bag. Fit for use instantly but better kept.

Unhurried barefoot boys, both black and white, head to a job site. Possibly Dalhousie Street.

Military Fare from Mrs. Kingsmill's Kitchen

Whether young Lt. Kingsmill's income was large enough to accommodate his wife at all his different postings, or whether she remained behind in Amherstburg, we do not know. However, in May, 1850, Lt. Kingsmill, commanding No. 6 Company, was ordered Montreal, then to St. John's. In January, 1853 he was promoted to Captain and posted back to Prescott in eastern Ontario. However, within three months of this new posting he was dead, of unrecorded reasons. His young widow, only 32, spent the remainder of her 28 years living on a British Government pension, alone in her house in Amherstburg.

The British army's very active involvement in India at this time explains the military taste for hot, spicy food.

CURRY POWDER*

[This makes 1 lb. curry powder. It produces a very pleasant, fairly hot powder, strongly flavoured with coriander.]

6 1/2 oz. coriander seed
1 1/2 oz. cumin
1 oz. Fenugreek
2 3/4 oz. black pepper
3/4 oz. cayenne pepper
3 oz. pale Turmeric
1/2 oz. best powdered ginger.

Finely grind each ingredient to a powder. Dry. Carefully mix together.

QUI-HI SAUCE*

[The ginger is pervasive in this pleasantly sharp condiment. The longer you leave it the more mellow it will become.]

2 oz. sharp apples, peeled and cored
2 oz. ripe tomatoes
2 oz. salt
2 oz. brown sugar
2 oz. raisins
1 oz. red chillies
1 oz. ground ginger
1/2 oz. garlic and 1/2 oz. shallots.

Pound all ingredients separately in a mortar using cayenne pepper if chillies not to be had. Mix all together and add 2 qts. cold vinegar. Place the jar containing this on a stove or by the side of a fire and stir it a few times a day for a month. Then strain but do not squeeze it dry. Bottle the liquor for sauce and put the thick residue, which is chutney, into jars. Secure it well.

The Emancipation Day Parade, Dalhousie Street, Amherstburg, August 1st, 1894

The Emancipation Day Parade

The Parade, brass band blaring and banners waving, marches up unpaved Dalhousie Street, a little way to the south of the fort. Dignified Mr. Bradley, riding crop gripped firmly, top hat shining in the August sun, leads the way on his handsome horse. Behind him comes the band, flanked by a flotilla of excited, mainly bare-foot, small boys. The Webber House on Dalhousie Street is still in existence, and the 5 and 10 cent store is, in the early 1990s, the Navy Yard Restaurant.

Traditionally, local bands marched down to the docks to welcome black families and friends arriving by boat from Detroit and Windsor, after which the crowd of up to 1000 would move to the town park for an afternoon of fun, food, music, and speeches, followed by a dance in the Town Hall after dark.

This happy day commemorated the abolition of slavery within the British Empire in 1833.

During the 1840s and 1850s, fugitive slaves took their chance crossing the river border between the United States and Canada. They would swim the river in summer if they could not gain passage, or, in winter, walk across the ice, often in family groups. So in Amherstburg and in the other riverside towns of Sandwich and Windsor, large black settlements of former slaves took root.

This old recipe was given to me by Mrs. Betty Simpson whose late husband Melvin founded the North American Black Historical Museum on King Street, in the heart of what was formerly the black settlement in Amherstburg. Next to the museum is the old Nazrey African Methodist Episcopal Church, built by former slaves in 1848, and now sadly in need of repair.

SWEET POTATO PIE

4 sweet potatoes
3 large eggs
2 T. butter (melted)
1 t. cinnamon
$1/2$ t. nutmeg
1 c. brown sugar
$1/2$ c. cream
$1/2$ t. salt
1 pie shell

Beat all ingredients together and pour into pie shell. Bake at 425°F for 15 minutes, then reduce heat to 400°F and bake for a further 30 minutes.

Return of Game that was [obtained?] Lieut Hutton — 34th Regt a[...]

Month 1839–40	Snipe			Woodcock			Quail			Duck			Partridge		
	Robertson	Hutton	others	Robertson	Hutton	others	Robertson	Hutton	others	Robertson	Hutton	others	Robertson	Hutton	others
April	146	110								9					
May															
June				131	83	83				1			7		
July				127	81	74									
August				7	19	22				11					
September	4	5	13		3	1	4	19	10	3	5				
October	65	13	2	1	52	7	21	111	58	4	3	1	1		5
November				2	1		127	58	47						2
December							5	45	25				1		
January							63								
February							16								
March		10									4				

Game table in Ensign Robertson's diary.

Shoot-em-up

Ensign Alexander Cunningham Robertson, recently arrived from England, and posted with his Regiment to Amherstburg due to rebel activity along the border, entered this table in his diary of the wildfowl shot throughout 1839 by his three friends, Captain Hammond, Lieutenant Hutton and Lieutenant Airey. Quite why he entered this is hard to understand, as he himself features not at all. Perhaps it was to impress his friends back home with the opportunities for sport shooting to be had in Canada all year round.

In fact, officers were encouraged by the army to shoot game, and spent much time doing so, to supplement the food served in the mess. And as the reedy marshes and flat country around Amherstburg is on one of the great migratory flight lines of North America, and home to thousands of birds, the officers must have dined well on what they shot.

Here is the recipe for a sauce to accompany wildfowl, given by a Captain Talbot to Mrs. Kingsmill.

SAUCE FOR WILD FOWL. CAPT. TALBOT,

A glass of port
$1/2$ t. mushroom catsup
$1/4$ t. cayenne pepper
1 anchovy
3 shallots chopped small
juice of $1/2$ lemon or an equal quantity vinegar.

Just over a year before Ensign Robertson entered the game table into his diary, he described a rebel action that took place near Windsor. Much of it involved racketing around Sandwich and Windsor in two horse wagons with a field gun, hunting for the enemy, while rumours flew. At one point, while firing at some rebels escaping in a boat, an American prisoner was brought to them. When they moved on towards Lake St. Clair, they left him in the charge of the local militia with orders not to hurt him. Returning at the end of the day, en route back to Sandwich, Robertson and his companions saw a dead man lying on his face by the roadside. It was their prisoner, shot "like a dog" by order of the militia colonel, John Prince, a local lawyer of a uniquely irascible nature. "4 or 5 people had already been served the same way." We shall meet Colonel John Prince again, up north in Sault Ste. Marie.

The Detroit River and Windsor shore with an American gunboat, possibly the Michigan, and the steamers Dove and Hope, in the foreground. Circa 1860.

The Serbs in Windsor

Across the Detroit River from the city of the same name is Windsor, Canada's southernmost city. Some of its streets still follow the long narrow outlines of the riverfront farms established by the earliest permanent settlers in Ontario, French *habitant* farmers who had arrived from Quebec in 1749. Windsor is now one of Canada's busiest cities with a population of infinite ethnic diversity.

As far back as 1910 records show a sprinkling of Serbs in Windsor, their names Anglicised though still recognizably Serb. In the mid 1920s about forty families and as many single men settled in the eastern municipality of Ford City, along Drouillard Road, within walking distance of the motor factories where many obtained work. Pavle Popov, who died in 1992 at nearly 91, was among them. "My father came on the boat in summer sandals," said his daughter, Illean Popov. "He remembers arriving on the train in Ford City in all this rain and slush. He got off at Drouillard Road — a mud road. It was raining cats and dogs. He didn't want to get off!" But "there were a few other Serbs and they looked after each other. If one had a job, he looked after the others." Three years later Pavle's wife and two children arrived. Illean remembers that "the family unit was very tight. We were happy. We were very poor, but we didn't know we were poor. Mother used to make candy for us with pumpkin seeds. She did a lot of baking." These early Serbs formed strong bonds within their community. Weekend get-togethers, plays, and picnics were happy times for all. Today the Serb Heritage Museum safeguards the memories and traditions of Windsor's Serbs.

CEVAPCICI

[Pronounced 'chevapcheechee' and customarily charcoal grilled on a barbecue.

2 T. butter or shortening
$1/2$ c. onion, finely chopped
2 garlic cloves, chopped
1 lb. beef, ground
1 lb. lamb or pork, ground
1 egg, lightly beaten
2 T. flour
salt, pepper, paprika to taste
1 T. parsley.

Heat butter in pan. Add onion and garlic and slightly brown. Transfer to a deep bowl. Add the remaining ingredients, combining well. Shape into 2 inch sausages, place on a plate, cover, and refrigerate for at least 2 hours before cooking. Grill for 15-20 minutes, turning over frequently to prevent sticking, till dark brown and thoroughly cooked through. Serve sprinkled with chopped onion or with an onion salad.

This and the recipe overleaf are compressed from ones in the Serbian cookbook *Prijatno,* produced in 1992 by the Circle of Serbian Sisters, Windsor.

Leaving behind the old land. Emigrants destined for Ontario manifest mixed emotions. Circa 1913

Serbs Preserve the Old Ways

The celebration of certain old traditions such as St. Sava's Day, January 27, and the Serbian Easter and Christmas, proved a source of strength and happiness to Windsor's early Serbs. One of the holiest days for a Serbian family is that of Krsna Slava (Patron Saint's Day). Each family has its own hereditary patron saint and on that saint's day the family dress in their Sunday best. Illean Popov described the ritual. "A candle is lit in the home and at the church. You make the kolac (Slava Bread), and boil the zito (sweet cooked wheat) and take it to the church where the priest cuts the kolac and blesses it. Then you take it home and whoever comes in has some of the wheat and a piece of the kolac."

SLAVSKI KOLAC [patron saint's day bread]

$^1/_2$ c. lukewarm milk, 2 T. sugar, 2 pgs. dry yeast.

5 egg yolks & 1 egg yolk
1 $^1/_2$ c. milk & 1 T. milk
$^1/_4$ c. sugar
$^1/_2$ c. butter
1 T. lemon rind
1 t. vanilla
$^1/_2$ t. salt
5 c. flour & $^1/_2$ c. flour
$^1/_4$ c. water.

Mix the yeast, the lukewarm milk, and the 2 T. sugar. Let rise 10-15 minutes. Combine the reserved egg yolk and 1 T. of milk and set aside for later use.

In a large bowl, well mix the 5 yolks and all other ingredients except the flour. Add yeast mix and combine well. Gradually add the 5 c. flour to make a firm dough. Knead till dough ceases to stick to the hands. Cover with a cloth and leave in a warm place to rise.

While this is rising, prepare the dough for decorating the bread by combining the remaining $^1/_2$ c. flour and the water and kneading it.

Following Serb tradition, into a portion of the dough press the seal mould for the symbol of Christ (seal mould may be purchased from the Serbian Orthodox Diocese, Mississauga). The remainder of the dough is formed into each family's traditional symbols such as a bible, cross, grapes, wheat, dove, or barrel. Set aside. When the yeast dough has doubled in size, roll out on a slightly floured board, divide it into seven and form balls. Grease and flour a round, deep pan (22x13 cm. or 9x4 inches). Place one ball in the centre of the pan, surround with the others and brush them with the reserved egg and milk mix. Decorate with the (unglazed) pastry symbols. Once again let rise till double. Bake at 350°F for 40 mins, then 300°F for 20 mins.

The building on King Street at Adelaide, Chatham, which housed the Provincial Freeman office. One of John Brown's meetings was held in the First Baptist Church barely visible to the left.

John Brown's Revolution

"John Brown's body lies a mouldrin' in the grave," runs the song that became the Battle hymn of the Republic in the Civil War. Brown, the fanatical abolitionist from Kansas, was sent to that grave in December, 1859, when he was hanged for treason after he led an abortive raid, part of his grand plan to destroy slavery, on the Arsenal at Harper's Ferry, West Virginia.

What is not so generally known is that it was in Chatham, a port on the River Thames in the flat fertile country of southwestern Ontario, that he planned and organised this raid. At that time a haven for freed and escaped slaves Chatham was a very logical place to head for, with his well disciplined group of "guerillas." Chatham resident Edwin Jones recalled seeing, as a child back in May 1858, "strangers carrying carpetbags coming from the depot . . . and the intent and compelling eyes of the white-bearded leader were disquieting." (From *Recollections*, Edwin Bassett Jones, privately published by Grace Jones Morgan, 1974.)

Meetings were held at which local black tradition maintains that Brown revealed plans to seize the U. S. Arsenal, arm his followers and march south, thereby triggering an uprising of slaves and enabling him to overthrow the Government. It is highly possible that the real work of formulating the plans occurred in the office of Isaac Shadd and his feisty sister, Mary Ann Shadd Cary, leading spirits in the black community, who ran the outspokenly anti-slavery newspaper, *The Provincial Freeman*. Brown was constantly seen in their office, along with other prominent black citizens of Chatham, by Warren Lambert, then a young printer's apprentice.

The recipe below (which strangely contains no ginger!) is that of a great-niece of Issac Shadd and Mary Ann Shadd Cary. It was given by her daughter, Gwendolyn Robinson, co-author with her husband John, of *Seek the Truth: A Story of Chatham's Black Community*.

CONSTANCE SHADD ROBBINS'S GINGERBREAD*

1/2 c. butter
1/2–3/4 c. molasses
1 c. brown sugar
2 eggs, beaten
2 c. flour, sifted
1/2 t. baking powder
pinch salt
1 t. baking soda
1 c. boiling water.

Warm together butter, molasses, and sugar until blended. Add to well beaten eggs. Mix in flour, baking powder and salt. Dissolve soda in boiling water and stir into mixture. This will be quite runny. Pour into prepared loaf tin. Bake in 310°F oven for about 1 hr. 50 mins.

King Street West, Chatham, 1860. The office of The Provincial Freeman was on King Street at Adelaid.

Harper's Ferry And After

A delay of 15 months fatally cooled local ardour in Chatham for John Brown's planned attack on Harper's Ferry, and when the call to arms finally came, only one Chatham black took part — young Osborne Perry Anderson, the Shadds' journeyman printer, who, according to fellow printer's apprentice, Warren Lambert, apparently drew lots with Isaac Shadd to see who would go. In fact, Anderson would be the only black in Brown's tiny company and one of the very few who escaped injury when a company of marines under Colonel Robert E. Lee arrived from Washington and promptly crushed the raid. Though briefly imprisoned, he made it back home within a few months. Lambert had a clear recollection of Anderson giving an address at a tea-meeting at a local church as "the only living representative of the Harper's Ferry Insurrection."

In later years he wrote, in conjunction with Mary Ann Shadd Cary, an account of his experiences, called A Voice from Harper's Ferry.

The country about Chatham is among the finest farmland in Ontario. Anna Jameson in the 1830s praised the town's position on the river and referred to the area as "literally flowing with milk and honey." If not precisely these products, the locality is certainly notable for excellent vegetables — asparagus, corn, and tomatoes in particular. Here is an old recipe for corn soup with a very delicate flavour, from a Chatham cookbook of the turn of the century. Be careful, if adding cream, not to submerge the subtle corn flavour.

CORN SOUP*

2 c. grated corn
2 c. water
1/2 onion, chopped finely
2-3 T. butter
1 1/2-2 T. flour
4 c. milk
salt and pepper to taste
whipped cream if wished

Cook corn in water till tender, then drain. Soften onion in a little of the butter, in a saucepan. Remove onion from pan. Melt remainder of butter, blend in flour, then add milk. Bring the milk nearly to a boil, then add corn, onion and seasoning to taste. Cook gently for a minute or two. A little whipped cream may be added before serving.

From the Beaver Mills Cook Book,
T. H. Taylor Co., Ltd.

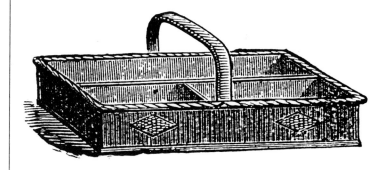

A group photograph of students at School Section # 13 Raleigh, North Buxton, 1910.

Learning To Go It Alone

For most slaves, after the initial euphoria of "freedom" had worn off, life in Canada tended to be one of bitter hardship, particularly in winter. Most had never had to look after themselves in the outside world and were ill-equipped to do so. Thoughtful men realised that these people needed help and education to support themselves.

Certainly this was the view of the Reverend William King. Born in Ireland and educated in Scotland, King migrated to North America with his parents and there married the daughter of a wealthy southern planter. With her and their two small children he returned to Edinburgh to study theology. Within two years his children and wife were dead, but King stayed in Edinburgh to finish his studies and then set out for Canada West (Ontario) to establish a settlement for escaped and freed black slaves.

Supported by the Governor General, Lord Elgin, he found good land in Raleigh Township near Chatham and (along with fourteen newly-freed slaves he had, to his embarrassment, inherited from his father-in-law) moved into what he named the Elgin Settlement.

He made farm lots available to black newcomers at low prices, and helped them farm and build their houses. A clause forbidding settlers to sell to whites for ten years helped forge a self-supporting community of black landowners and with this came political clout. Soon black settlers began to establish small industries around Buxton. Due to a happy combination of sound financing and thoughtful organisation, the settlement became Canada's most successful self-supporting black community. Population peaked at 1000 in 1856, but in the aftermath of the civil war many settlers chose to return to the south to rejoin their families.

The first church-school in Buxton village, paid for by King himself, was soon recognised as offering a higher standard of education than the local government school and numbers of white families sought to enter their children in it. The 1910 photograph opposite shows a later Buxton school, by this time amalgamated with the local public school. In the back row, fourth from the left, stands Sydney Prince. The following recipe is from his wife, Minetta, who became a pioneer in the west in later life. It was given to me by Shannon Prince.

MRS. MINETTA PRINCE'S DROP COOKIES*

$1/2$ c. butter
1 c. brown sugar
2 eggs, beaten
$1/2$ heaped t. soda
$1/6$ c. hot water
1 $3/4$ c. flour
$1/2$ t. cinnamon
$1/2$ t. nutmeg,
$1/4$ t. cloves
1 c. chopped nuts, dates, raisins, coconut.

Set oven to 375°F. Sift flour and spices. Cream butter and sugar. Add eggs. Stir soda in water, then add. Blend in flour, then nuts, fruit. Drop with spoon on baking sheet. Bake 15 mins. [Makes about 30 cookies]

"Bread and cheesemaker." A cheese-making mill in York, near Union, south of St. Thomas.

The Eccentric Colonel Talbot

On the Talbot Trail between Wallacetown and Fingal is a cairn on the south side of Highway 16. It commemorates the settlement created by one of early Ontario's most colourful and fascinating characters, Lt. Colonel the Hon. Thomas Talbot, after whom St. Thomas was named. Born into a large family of impecunious Irish aristocrats in 1771, he was commissioned in the army by the age of eleven. At sixteen, handsome, amusing and lively, he became Aide-de-Camp to his relative, the Marquis of Buckingham, Lord Lieutenant of Ireland. Four years later, Talbot was sent out to Upper Canada as Aide to its first Lieutenant Governor, John Graves Simcoe. After another posting, and promotion to Lt. Colonel at twenty-five, Talbot left the army, obtained an extensive grant of land in the vast forests north of Lake Erie with a view to founding a colony, and returned to Upper Canada.

In 1803, turning his back on civilised society, he built himself a log hut at the top of a cliff on the forest shore and settled there (the commemorative cairn mentioned above indicates the site). For sixteen terrible years while he cleared the land, his only companions were twenty rough labourers. His brother, on visiting him, exclaimed in dismay, "All I heard of you being a recluse in a log hut and your own bread and cheesemaker and your own cow-milker, is too true." However, by 1837, the Talbot Settlement contained approximately 650,000 acres of land, with about 50,000 people settled in 28 townships.

Employing distinctly controversial practises, Talbot ran his virtual principality for nearly fifty years, and was notable in later life for an extraordinary mixture of charm and eccentric curmudgeonliness. His odd garb (an ancient yellow-dyed sheepskin coat and cap) and personal mannerisms excited greatly conflicting reactions.

As his brother had lamented, Talbot made his own cheese and prided himself on his home-made bread. Here is a steamed bread from Sparta, near St. Thomas.

NUT BROWN BREAD*

[a rich textured cake-bread tasting strongly of molasses]

2 c. graham flour
1 c. sour milk
1 t. baking soda
$^1/_2$ c. raisins
1 c. chopped nuts
$^1/_2$ c. molasses.

Combine ingredients. Put in buttered bowl, cover with strong wax paper and tie down. Steam 1 $^1/_2$ hours. Remove wax paper and bake 10 minutes or more at 350°F. From *The Spartan Cook Book* produced by The Sparta Women's Temperance Auxiliary (a Quaker group), 1908. One wonders what Talbot would have made of this source! He had given short shrift to the temperance lecturer, Dr. Goodhue, when called upon by that gentleman.

Geese climb a bank in a recently cleared area.

Primitive Ways

"About five o'clock we reached St. Thomas, one of the prettiest places I had ever seen . . . The view from it, over a fertile, well settled country, is very beautiful and cheering. The place bears the Christian name of Colonel Talbot, who styles it his capital . . ."

Anna Jameson,
Winter Studies and Summer Rambles in Canada, 1838.

The naming of St. Thomas after him may well have appealed to Talbot's sense of humour, as he had little of the saint about him. It is said that on Sundays he would read Divine Service to his assembled settlers and afterwards, as wine was an expensive commodity in those parts, a whisky bottle was passed round to ensure no falling off in the settlers' devotions.

Talbot not only made his own whisky in large amounts on his 600-acre property, but raised his own geese, chickens, ducks, and turkeys which he plucked himself for the table.

TO ROAST AN OLD FOWL

Neatly dress the fowl and soak in cold water for 2 hours. Boil until tender. Stuff with sage dressing and place in roaster. Mix 2 T. flour with butter and spread over the chicken. Bake in a moderate oven till a delicate brown.

From the *St. Thomas Y.W.C.A. Cook Book*, 1908.

CHESTNUT STUFFING FOR TURKEY

6 c. chestnuts
2 T. butter
2 t. salt
1/4 t. pepper.

Shell chestnuts. Place in hot water and boil till skins are soft. Drain and remove skins. Replace the chestnuts in fresh boiling water [or stock] and boil till soft. Remove from heat. While hot, press through a colander, a few at a time. Add butter and seasoning.

From the *St. Thomas Y. W. C. A. Cook Book*, 1908.

A man surveys his domain at the door of his log house, axe and gun to hand.

"The Old Buffalo In His Lair"

"... I had heard of his singular manners, of his being a sort of woman-hater, who had not for thirty years allowed a female to appear in his sight," wrote Anna Jameson, of her imminent visit to Talbot. "However, putting my trust in Providence, I prepared to encounter the old buffalo in his lair." Talbot was in fact charming to Mrs. Jameson. Five years before Mrs. Jameson's visit, Talbot had built himself a larger house. It was much more pretentious than his first but visitors still spoke of its "primitive simplicity."

"The front door ... opened into a large store room or vestibule crowded with piles of homespun blankets, ... sacks of grain, sheepskins and barrels of flour, with an occasional hen hatching her eggs in an empty barrel.

"Here Talbot kept his ... famed sheepskin coat and cap; and from it he carried feed to the poultry that swarmed about the yard and roosted on the verandah among the dogs. From the rafters .. hung various farm implements, and even on occasion, a dead wildcat," as Mrs. Jameson encountered to her horror.

Talbot in fact seems to have enjoyed company, but very much on his own terms. One devout dinner guest, about to bow his head in prayer preparatory to his meal, was shocked to see his host already tucking in. He requested a delay to give thanks. "Well be damned quick about it," Talbot shot back with his usual grace.

A GENUINE IRISH STEW*

[Talbot could have provided everything for this extremely basic stew except the seasonings.]

2 lbs. mutton chops from best end of neck
4 $1/4$ lbs. potatoes
8 large onions
plenty of seasoning
strong beef stock.

In a stew pan, densely layer up half the peeled, sliced potatoes and onions, then all the meat, well seasoned with pepper and a little salt. Top with remaining onion-potato mix. Add stock just to cover. Cover tightly and simmer 3 hours at 250°F.

From the *St. Thomas Y. W. C. A. Cook Book,* 1908.

33

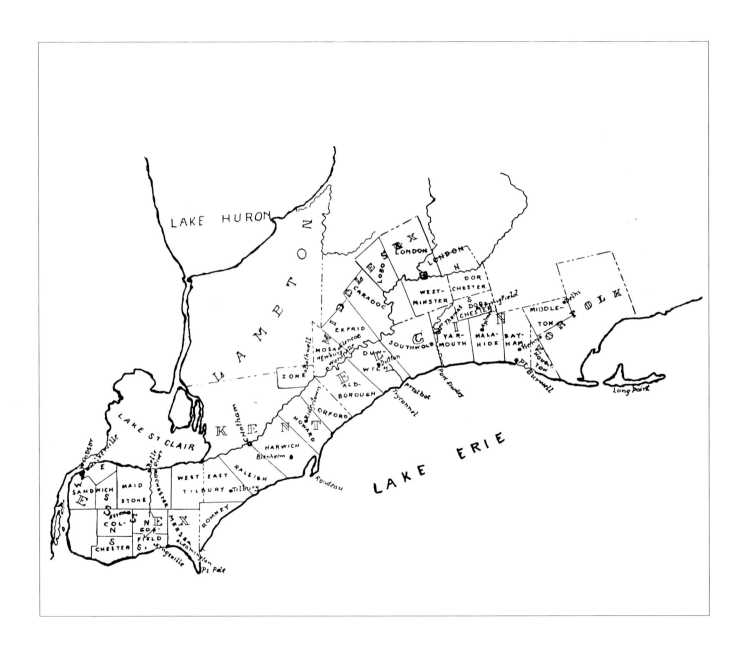

An old map showing the Talbot Settlement.

The Anniversary Dinner

"Colonel Talbot," wrote Anna Jameson, "never associated with the people except on one grand occasion, the anniversary of the foundation of his settlement." This was held at St. Thomas and attended by only the most respectable settlers. "The colonel himself opens the ball with one of the ladies, generally showing his taste by selecting the youngest and prettiest."

May 21, the day in 1803 on which Talbot felled the first tree, was celebrated by the settlers until 1847. In 1828, the Anniversary ball was held in the Talbot Hotel which was massed with flowers for the "sumptuous entertainment." Here is part of the report for the event which began at what certainly seems to modern party-goers the astonishing hour of 4 p. m., "when all sat down to an immense table . . . . The ladies made a gay appearance, some of them decked with wreaths and garlands of native flowers, exhibiting a most charming display of sylvan innocence. Dancing commenced at half past eight, and continued till 'fair Aurora burst her golden ray.' Each seemed emulous to equal the cordiality of others, and the utmost pleasantry and conviviality prevailed throughout."

In 1903 the event was revived to celebrate the Centenary of the Talbot Settlement. Below is a local recipe which might have been served.

DRIED APPLE CAKE*

[Kissing cousin to a gingerbread, this cake bread is distinguished by golden syrup and dried apples.]

3 c. dried apples
2 c. syrup
2 eggs
1 c. sugar
1 c. milk
1/2 c. butter, softened
1 t. bicarb. of soda
3 c. flour
spices.

Soak apples overnight in water. Chop lightly. Simmer in syrup for 1 1/2 hours. Cool. Beat eggs; add sugar and milk. Beat in butter. Sift flour, soda and spices (1 t. each cinnamon and cloves), and add to egg mixture. Finally add apples. Combine well. Pour into two greased 5x9x2 inch pans. Bake at 325°F for 1 hour.

From *The Spartan Cook Book*, Sparta, 1908.

King Street East, Ingersoll. 1872.

Queen for Cheese

"The next place we came to was Oxford, or rather, Ingersoll [Oxford was re-named Ingersoll by the brothers of Laura Secord, heroine of the war of 1812, in memory of their father, Thomas Ingersoll], . . . It is a little village, presenting the usual sawmill, grocery store and tavern, with a dozen shanties congregated on the bank of the stream."

Anna Jameson,
Winter Studies and Summer Rambles in Canada, 1838.

Ingersoll is situated about 120 kilometres northeast of St. Thomas. Thirty-five years after Mrs. Jameson's visit it had changed considerably, as witness the attractive buildings opposite. At least part of its increased prosperity was due to the emergence of the cheese-making industry after 1865 when James Harris built the Ingersoll Cheese Factory. Harris prospered and soon built himself a fine Italianate, yellow-brick house, Elm Hurst, which can still be seen from Highway 401. To publicize the infant industry, Harris and other Oxford County farmers co-operated to make a gigantic cheese, 21 feet in circumference and weighing 7,300 pounds, which was exhibited in Toronto, New York, and London, England. James McIntyre, a coffin maker, known as the Ingersoll Poet, was moved to verse at the sight of it:

We have seen thee, Queen of cheese,
Lying quietly at your ease,
Gently fanned by evening breeze,
Thy fair form no flies dare seize.
All gaily dressed soon you'll go
To the great Provincial Show,
To be admired by many a beau
In the city of Toronto.
Cows numerous as a swarm of bees,
Or as the leaves upon the trees,
It did require to make thee please,
And stand unrivalled, queen of cheese.

Plainly, Ingersoll was much stronger on cheese than poets.

INGERSOLL STUFFED CELERY*

4 T. cream cheese
1 pimento
4 large olives
1 bunch celery.

Wash celery. Mash cheese, pimento and olives. Pack hollow of celery stalks with mixture. Garnish with young celery leaves.

From *Ingersoll Recipes,* pre-1925.

A girl milking cows in the farm yard.

A Great Cheese-Making Place

Eight years after the monster Queen of cheese was created, in July, 1874, Lord and Lady Dufferin, the Governor General and his wife, visited Ingersoll near the end of a six-week "Western" tour. Lady Dufferin describes the visit in her journal:

"On to Ingersoll, a great cheese-making place. There was an arch made of cheeses, the motto being, 'Cheese, the making of Canada.' We drove out in procession to a cheese-factory and saw the whole process of converting new milk into cheese in five hours . . . . One large cheese, on being cut into, was found to contain numerous bottles of champagne." No doubt Lady Dufferin, who had a great sense of humour, enjoyed it all immensely.

Here is another recipe for cheese, found in Ingersoll.

CHEESE SOUFFLE

2 T. butter
3 T. flour
$^1/_2$ c. milk
$^1/_2$ t. salt
3 eggs, separated
few grains cayenne
$^1/_3$ c. cheese, grated.

Make cheese sauce using butter, flour, milk and cheese. Season. Add beaten egg yolks, and when mixture is cold, fold in the stiffly beaten egg whites. Pour into a buttered baking dish and bake 20 minutes in a slow oven.

From *Why and How to Use Cheese*, 1925.

Peddlers selling crates of Gunn's eggs and bolts of fabric help a customer near Wingham, 1905.

The 35,000-egg Wingham Omelette

A detour northwards, to the agricultural hinterland behind Goderich, brings us to Wingham, a remote hamlet until the railway's arrival in 1870 made it a busy centre for local farm goods. On April 10, 1902, the front page of the *Wingham Advance* announced that "the produce business of the late Charles Gillespie [on the north side of Alfred Street] has been bought by the well known firm of D. Gunn Bros. of Toronto, and the business will now be known as the Wingham Produce Co. , which will be under the management of Mr. Chas. J. Graham . . . . we understand (he) is an expert pickler. . ." And so he might well have been as D. Gunn Bros. (later amalgamated into Canada Packer's Co. Ltd.) was the largest exporter of pickled eggs to Britain, and the largest handler of eggs in Canada. Unfortunately, two years later, a fire sent both the building and 35,000 eggs up in flames. Following are some egg recipes found in Wingham.

OMELET O'BRIEN*

[A tasty light supper dish. Serves 2 or 3]

2 T. butter
4 t. chopped onion
1 large green pepper, chopped
1 tomato, skinned and chopped
4 slices bacon
1 t. salt
pepper
6 eggs
seasoning

Fry bacon till barely crisp. Drain, reserving fat. Melt butter in saucepan. Add onion. Cook till tender. Add green pepper and cook gently 10 minutes, then add tomato and seasoning and continue cooking a further 10 mins. With eggs and seasoning make an omelette, using bacon fat instead of butter. Pour pepper mixture round it, and garnish with bacon.

From *The Art of Cooking Made Easy*, post 1913. "Obtainable from J. W. Mckibbon's Drugstore in Wingham for 25 cents."

A crowded poultry yard in Colborne Township, not far from Wingham.

Wingham & Eggs

APPLE OMELET*

Serve with broiled spare rib or roast pork. [This is really a tight-textured applesauce rather than an omelette, but very pleasant used as suggested.]

9 large tart apples, peeled, cored
4 eggs, beaten
1 c. sugar
1 T. butter
cinnamon, cloves or nutmeg.

Stew apples till very soft. Puree, and while warm mix in butter and sugar. Cool. Add eggs, and pour into shallow baking dish. Bake in 350°F degree oven till done.

From *The Art of Cooking Made Easy*, 1913 or later.

SCRIPTURE CAKE

[This recipe came from the Wingham Advance, *October 30, 1902. We have corrected a few wrong references, re-arranged the listing of ingredients to make baking sense and added some more 'down-to-earth' instructions. Should this prove less than divine, complain to a higher authority.]*

2 ½ c. Judges V, 25 (butter)
2 c. Jeremiah VI, 20 (fine sugar)
6 Jeremiah XVII, 11 (eggs)
4 ½ c. 1 Kings IV, 22 (flour)
½ c. Judges IV, 19 (milk)
2 c. 1 Samuel XXX, 12 (raisins)
2 c. Nahum III, 12 (figs)
1 c. Numbers XVII, 8 (almonds)
2 T. 1 Samuel XIV, 25 (honey)
Season with 2 Chronicles IX, 9 (spice)
Pinch Leviticus II, 13 (salt)
3 t. Amos IV, 5 (baking powder).

Follow Solomon's prescription for making a good child (Proverbs XXIII, 14) and you will have a good cake.
Would it were as simple as that!
Switch oven to 300°F. Sift flour. Grease and line cake tin. Chop fruit and mix a little of the flour with it. Cream butter and sugar well. Beat in eggs singly, alternating with 1 T. of the flour. Add milk. Beat well. Add fruit and almonds, honey, spice and salt. Blend in remaining flour sifted with baking powder. Pour into tin. Bake in lower part of oven for 1 ¼ hrs. or till done.

John Mitchell stands among his apple trees, Thornbury, 1930s.

Thornbury, Apples, & The Mitchells

Northeast of Wingham lies Georgian Bay. In mid May, 1991, the countryside on its south shore was foamy with apple blossom. Jack Mitchell, decended from a long line of remarkably tall apple men, stood outside his house on the Beaver River and faced north into the breeze blowing gently off Nottawasaga Bay. He was talking in his calm manner about the extraordinary mini-climate of the Thornbury area.

"Do you feel that wind?" he asked. "The temperature is moderated here adjacent to the Georgian Bay, inland for about four miles. In the fall and spring — the danger periods — the prevailing winds are off the water and the water is much warmer than the air. Ninety-five per cent of the orchards are within three miles of the lake at the outside. Northern Spys are definitely the best apple around here. For apple sauce or pies. It's one of the old, old varieties — even older than Macintoshes. [These two] probably grow better here than anywhere in the world."

Jack Mitchell was born in Clarksburg and has spent his life in the apple business, as did his father and grandfather before him. His Scottish great-grandparents arrived in the area in 1849 and bought a 200-acre farm. Of their twelve children only two girls and five boys survived. One of these was Jack's grandfather, John (opposite), one of the first farmer entrepreneurs. Sensing the area's potential for apple-growing, John bought a 50-acre farm where 10th Line intersects the Clarksburg sideroad (the old cedar-shingled Mitchell farmhouse was designated an historic building recently), and exclusively grew apples. For its time, it was a very large orchard. Then, in 1905, he organised a company called The Georgian Bay Fruit Growers, with the apple farm as part of its holdings, and bought another 400 acres of orchards. "And that", said grandson Jack, "was the origin of the business."

In the 1920s, two-thirds of the apple crop was shipped to Liverpool in barrels. Later still, canned apple juice and apple sauce appeared under the brand name, Mitchell's. Soon the 450 acres of apples could not keep up with the canning demand so the whole area began to sell apples to the firm. "I even brought several car-loads from Nova Scotia one year when we had a light crop," Jack admits, almost as if confessing to infidelity.

"We sold the business in 1970 and I've been retired ever since. But I still have apple orchards." It seems once an apple man, always an apple man.

A huge pile of apples, Clarksburg.

Deep in the Core of Apple Country

Jack provided this Mitchell recipe and commented, "This is the most tasty doggone apple recipe I ever came across." He recommended using Ida Red or Northern Spys for it and produced a utensil resembling a miniature waggon wheel with which to quickly section apples into eighths.

APPLE CRISP*

[Everything Jack says it is!]

6 – 8 large tart apples, peeled & cored
1 t. cinnamon
1 c. brown sugar
1 c. white sugar
1 c. flour
1 egg, beaten
1/2 t. salt
1 t. baking powder
chopped walnuts
1/2 c. melted butter.

Section the apples into eighths. Place in a 9x9x3 inch greased pan. Switch oven to 350°F. Mix the cinnamon and brown sugar and sprinkle apples with half. Combine the white sugar, flour, egg, salt and baking powder and spread over the apples. Sprinkle walnuts over this, then the remaining cinnamon mix. Over the top, pour the melted butter. Bake in the oven for 40 mins.

Mary Armstrong is another with deep roots in this region. Her grandfather, Henry McRae, a Scot from Lower Canada, settled in Heathcote, clearing land which her father also farmed, only ten miles south of where Mary now lives. Her own farm, on the outskirts of Clarksburg, is islanded in a sea of apple trees. The characteristics of each variety are so familiar to her that she adjusts the flavourings with every apple.

The following recipe is from a book which belonged to Mary's Irish grandmother, who arrived in the area aged nineteen. The book has no date, but Mary remembers her grandmother serving this to her as a small child.

TAPIOCA AND APPLES

Soak 1 c. tapioca in 4 c. water for 2 hours. Peel and core as many sour apples as will fit the bottom of a buttered baking dish. Fill the cavity of the apples with butter, sugar and cinnamon. Turn the tapioca over the apples and bake till done. Serve with the following hard sauce.

HARD SAUCE

Beat the yolks of 1 or 2 eggs till light; add sufficient sugar to make stiff; beat until smooth and creamy; flavour to suit taste.

From *The Beaver Valley Collection – of the Latest and Best Recipes. Compiled by the Ladies of St. Paul's Presbyterian Church, Thornbury.*

Sir Allan MacNab, to the right of the two ladies in white, entertains the visiting English directors of the Great Western Railway at Dundurn Castle, Hamilton, c. 1860. Senator Donald MacInnes is fifth from his right.

The "Well-to-Do" Scots

"Hamilton is of a decidedly Scottish character, Gaelic is often heard in its streets, but not to so great an extent as the Saxon Doric of the Lowlands. The names over the shop doors smack of Sutherlandshire, Invernessshire, and Argyllshire. There are a few Germans and Irish . . . but the predominating race is the Scotch - the greater part of them thriving and well-to-do persons."

> Charles Mackay, a Scottish visitor writing in *Early Travellers in The Canadas*, 1858.

"It is a very prettily situated town . . . All the streets are planted with trees, and there is a high hill behind the town, from which the view is magnificent. . . We are staying with Mr. McInnes [sic] who makes us very comfortable."

> Lady Dufferin in 1872, as a guest of Dundurn Castle's second owner, Senator Donald MacInnes.

In the nineteenth century, important visitors to Niagara Falls often stayed nearby at Dundurn Castle. Twelve years before Lord and Lady Dufferin's visit, its builder, Sir Allan MacNab, entertained the Prince of Wales there on his return from the Falls. MacNab had been Prime Minister of the united Canadas for two years. The handsome home he built had a beautiful view overlooking the harbour and eventually of the railway, of which he was a director. Aesthetic or not, the railway would enormously stimulate Hamilton's prosperity, linking it with major ports and markets in New York, Buffalo, Pennsylvania, and Chicago.

NEW COCK-A-LEEKIE SOUP

[The prunes are traditional in this Edinburgh soup.]

2 lbs. veal cutlet or fowl
$1/4$ lb. butter
2 onions, sliced
$1/4$ lb. lean bacon
3 cloves
2 t. salt
1 t. sugar
$1/2$ t. pepper
$1/2$ c. & 10 c. water
2 lbs. leeks
4 qts. water
18 fresh prunes

Cut flesh into pieces. Put in pan with next seven ingredients and $1/2$ c. water. Cook, turning over till a white glaze forms at the bottom. Add 10 c. water. Simmer 30 mins. Pass through a sieve and save best pieces of meat. Meantime, blanch the white parts of leek for 10 mins. in 4 qts. water. Drain. Boil the stock and half the leeks together till reduced by half. Add other half of leeks, meat and prunes. Simmer $1/2$ hr. and serve.

From *The Canadian Housewife's Manual of Cookery*, Published by Henry I. Richards. Printer, *Spectator* office, Hamilton, 1861.

Fruit wagons and vendors crowd the Market, Hamilton, early 20th century .

Tomatoes in the Back Yard

"Hamilton was very Scottish back then, and Irish and English," says Tina Florio, about her family's arrival in Hamilton. "They looked down on us. This went on a long time. When my sisters went to work they had to go down Bay Street, over the bridge, to the cotton mills on MacNab street. At the corner of Stewart Street there would be a group of men with baseball bats, to beat up the Italians. My father used to take the girls to work - 6 o'clock every morning. This was 1915."

Her father, Francesco (Frank) Campanella, was one of a huge wave of Italians who emigrated to Canada in 1903. Frank left behind a wife and son, twin girls and another girl. He got work in a steel company — backbreaking, dirty work — but there were constant lay-offs. It took him seven years to save the money to bring his family over from Sicily. The boy died in the interim.

"When the family arrived, all the acquaintances and near relatives got together and rented this great big clapboard home and they all lived together. Their main meal was always macaroni. Before they went to bed, whoever's turn it was, she made the macaroni, and spread it on the table, and that was for the next day's big meal. If they didn't have tomatoes — which they couldn't afford — it was salt, pepper and a little olive oil, and home made bread. In the summer they'd grow tomatoes in the back yard. They grew everything you could imagine.

"After the [First World] war steel jobs were unavailable, so my father bought a horse and wagon to sell fruit door-to-door in the outskirts. Hamilton ended at Ottawa Street. Then it was nothing but mud and farms. I was little but I loved to help, and when he'd come home we'd put newspapers in the kitchen door and take his boots off there, and I'd clean them. It was hard but we made it. Hard work and family co-operation is the backbone of our lives.

"My father loved this country. He never wanted to go back. He used to always say, 'I've come into heaven.'"

TINA FLORIO'S TOMATO SAUCE

[Originally, of course, fresh tomatoes were used. But cans of whole and crushed ones appeared before the turn of the century, and save a great deal of labour. The sauce freezes beautifully.]

1 28-oz can plum tomatoes
1 28-oz. can crushed tomatoes
1 medium onion, finely chopped
2 cloves garlic
a little olive oil
basil, mint, oregano
1 level T. salt
crushed hot peppers to taste.

Simmer about 1 hr. or till thick. Fry spareribs and put them in the sauce.

Women jostle to see the Prince of Wales (centre, in light trousers, knee bent) at Niagara Falls, 1860.

The Prince, the Ladies & the Falls

In 1860 the 18-year-old Albert Edward, Prince of Wales, arrived in Canada for a tour of British North America. Still slim and beardless, it is hard to recognize in him the future King Edward VII. For the prince it was probably a great delight, an escape from the unremitting disapproval of his mother, Victoria, and his hated studies at Oxford (Professor Goldwin Smith: "I tried to teach him history, but only succeeded in teaching him whist"). Furthermore, the witty and high-spirited prince found himself the centre of a great deal of rapturous attention, particularly from the young ladies.

Gardner Englehart was private secretary to the Duke of Newcastle, tour adviser on the trip. The following is from his account of the Niagara Falls visit:

"14 September, 1860 [en route to Niagara Falls on the Great Western Railway]. Our hats, which had been deposited in a dressing room during luncheon (at Brantford) were found to be denuded of their bands. The prince was the first to discover this in the train — we at once came to the conclusion that [the culprits were] his enthusiastic admirers, the young ladies, determined to possess some relic of him."

Certainly, in the photograph, the only hat sporting a band seems to be that of General Bruce, at the extreme left. It would have mattered to the prince - he was a dandy. In fact, in later years his nephew the Kaiser called him "The old peacock."

A search for old Niagara Falls recipes proved fruitless. As one who knows about these things said, "Niagara Falls doesn't conserve its past unless it went over the falls in a barrel." Instead, in *The Watford Methodist*

Church Ladies' Cook Book, produced in Watford in 1904, I found several recipes connected to Albert Edward (who dropped the Albert on becoming King).

Albert Edward had an incurable weakness for beautiful women. One of the most famous was Lillie Langtry, born in the island of Jersey in the Channel Islands and known as the Jersey Lily.

JERSEY LILY CAKE*

[An excellent, tight-textured, white cake, with some fruit and nuts.]

1/2 c. butter, softened
1 c. fruit sugar
1/2 c. milk
2 c. cake and pastry flour
2 t. baking powder
1/2 c. raisins
1/2 c. walnuts
whites of 4 eggs.

Grease and line a cake tin. Sift flour and baking powder. Stiffly beat egg whites. Cream butter well, then add sugar, and cream thoroughly. Add fruit and nuts. Switch oven to 285°F. Add milk by degrees, alternating with a small amount of the flour. Blend in remaining flour, and fold in stiff egg whites. Pour into cake tin. Bake for 2 hours to 2 hours and 25 mins, or until tester comes out clean.

Visitors view Niagara Falls.

View Points & Points Of View

"I have no words for my utter disappointment . . . . "
Anna Jameson, *Winter Studies in Canada,* 1837.

"It was not until I came on Table Rock, and looked — Great Heaven, on what a fall of bright green water! — that it came upon me in its' full might and majesty."
——Charles Dickens, *American Notes* 1842.

"I know no other one thing so beautiful, so glorious, and so powerful . . . ."
——Anthony Trollope, *North America,* 1861.

"I was surprised to find we were expected to array ourselves in yellow oilskin trousers with jackets and hoods of the same material. . We did look a funny yellow party, dripping with water."
——Lady Dufferin, wife of the Governor General, in *My Canadian Journal,* 1872.

"I was disappointed with Niagara . . most people must be . . . Every American bride is taken there, and the sight of the stupendous waterfall must be one of the earliest if not the keenest, disappointments in American married life."
——Oscar Wilde, May, 1882.

The following, from the *Watford Church Ladies' Cook Book* (Watford, 1904), is an odd cake, perhaps illustrative of the tastes of the time. It is composed of two completely different cakes one atop the other. The dark part is spicy and tight textured while the light part is a mild, creamy-white cake.

PRINCE OF WALES CAKE*

Dark Part:
scant $1/2$ c. butter, 1 c. brown sugar
yolks of 3 eggs
1 c. raisins, dredged with flour
1 T. molasses
2 c. flour, sifted,
$1/2$ c. sour milk
1 t. nutmeg, 1 t. cloves
1 t. soda

Cream butter; then add sugar, beating well. Add egg yolks singly, with a spoonful of the flour. Beat well, and add raisins. Slowly pour in molasses and milk, with a small amount of the flour. Sieve in remaining flour, with spices and soda. Mix well. Pour into prepared straight-sided pan and bake at 350°F for about 1 hour.

White Part:
1 c. flour, $1/2$ c. cornstarch
scant $1/2$ c. butter, softened,
1 c. granulated sugar
$1/2$ c. milk
2 t. baking powder.
3 egg whites, stiffly beaten,

Sift flour and cornstarch. Rub in butter. Blend in sugar. Mix milk with baking powder and combine well. Fold in egg whites. Pour into prepared pan. Bake at 350°F for about 1 hr. No instructions were provided for icing, so I suggest a sandwich of caramel icing or jam sandwich, and almond icing over-all.

Blondin walks across the Niagara Gorge, carrying his manager on his back, September, 1860.

Teddy & The Tight Rope Walker

The great trapeze artist, Blondin, whose real name was Jean François Gravelet, walked across the Gorge on a tight-rope three times in 1859, and repeated his feat in 1860 at the time of the Prince of Wales's visit to Niagara Falls. The following is Gardner Englehart's account:

". . . We (returned) to the bridge in time to see Blondin cross his rope, 1,600 feet long, stretched across the gulf immediately below the bridge. He afterwards carried over a man upon his back and then crossed alone on stilts! The Prince remonstrated against this last performance but he persisted."

"18 September. We left this, the most charming and wonderful spot in Canada at 9.30. . . ."

Young midshipman Thomas Bunbury Gough, R.N., who knew about these things, averred that "[Blondin's rope] was a white Manila one, two inches in diameter, and drawn as taut as could be." Gough was off Her Majesty's yacht *Hero* which had transported the Prince to Canada, and was on leave with other young midshipmen, watching the scene in the crowd.

Albert Edward ("Bertie" to his family and "Good old Teddy" to the delighted populace) had to wait forty years for the succession, becoming King in 1901. This most congenial, warm-hearted and tactful of princes loved a good time. "Guttural and gluttonous Bertie" an unkind newspaper called him once, referring to his self-indulgence and the fact that he spoke with a slight German accent, acquired from his father. And it is true that, fuelled by endless cigars, champagne and good food, he spun on an endless quest for entertainment.

CHAMPAGNE CUP

[Teddy would probably have preferred his straight.]

1/4 bottle champagne
2 bottles soda
1 liqueur glass brandy
2 T. powdered sugar
a few thin strips cucumber rind
ice.

Mix just before use.

From *The Home Cook Book*, Toronto, 1887.

The Duke and Duchess of York on the verandah of the Queen's Royal Hotel, Niagara-on-the-Lake, 1901.

The Duke Sits It Out

Forty-one years later, on October 12, 1901, good breeding must indeed have been put to the test. The occasion was the arrival at the Queen's Royal Hotel at Niagara-on-the-Lake of Teddy's son and daughter-in-law, the Duke and Duchess of Cornwall and York (the future King George V and Queen Mary). As Joy Ormsby tells it in her article on the hotel in the *Niagara Advance*. They were on the return leg of a Royal Tour, with Lord and Lady Minto and retinue. In honour of their Highnesses the hotel installed the last word in new technology, an acetylene gas plant to light the building. Unfortunately, to the management's utter horror, inexperience with the plant caused a gas leak. While gas was being cleared from the rooms the Royals waited on the verandah. There they sat, and sat, and sat, the overhead flags shifting uneasily, till 3 o'clock in the morning when it was safe for them to enter.

The hotel has long gone. A gazebo in a pretty park, where the Niagara River joins Lake Ontario, occupies its once commanding site. Built around 1869, and originally named "The Royal Niagara," the hotel was in its heyday at the time of the Royal visit, with a short but highly social season. Sadly, its popularity dwindled after the First World War and it was sold in 1921. When its decline still continued, it was demolished in 1930 and its grounds turned into a park.

What would have been offered by an anxious staff to a Royal party, waiting patiently on a mid-October night till 3 a.m.? No doubt drinks were served. Certainly Minto, at front left, looks badly in need of one (the Duke could be irritable). Perhaps the staff served whisky or a hot wine Sangaree and hot lemonade, served with the hotel's own excellent Lemon Fruit cake.

WINE SANGAREE*

[a warm, soothing drink]

In a glass combine $1/2$ c. Port or Madeira, $1/2$ c. hot water, 1 t. or sugar to taste and a dusting of nutmeg.

This, and the recipe below is from *Every Lady's Book*, Niagara-on-the-Lake, 1846.

LEMONADE (SYRUP)*

[strong but good]

Peel 6 lemons. Squeeze juice from them and add $1/2$ lb. fine sugar. Pour a little boiling water over the peels and cover securely. When cold, strain into the lemon juice and sugar. Bottle syrup and make up with hot water in winter or ice water in summer in the proportion of one wine-glass of this to $3/4$ tumbler of water.

THE QUEEN'S,

BREAKFAST.

FRUIT.

Oatmeal Porridge.

OYSTERS.

Fried.   Stewed.   Raw.

Green Tea.   Black Tea.   Coffee.   Chocolate.

FISH.

Broiled Fresh Fish.   Loch Fyne Herring.
Cod Fish Balls.   Salt Mackerel.
Yarmouth Bloater.   Finnan Haddie.

BROILED.

Beefsteak, Plain and with Onions.
St. Louis Sugar-cured Ham. Mutton Chops. Pork Chops, Plain and with Onions.
Kidneys.   Glasgow Beef Ham.   Park's Breakfast Bacon.
Tripe.   Pig's Feet.

FRIED.

Mutton Cutlets, Breaded.   Liver and Bacon.   Veal Cutlets, Breaded.
Beef Hash.   Tripe.   Sausage.

STEWED.

Codfish, Cream Sauce.   Kidney

POTATOES.

Baked.   Fried.   Stewed.   Saratoga Chips.   Minced.   Boiled.   Lyonnaise.

MISCELLANEOUS.

White Bread.   Brown Bread.   Dry Toast.   Buttered Toast.   Milk Toast.
French Rolls.   Graham Rolls.   Corn Bread.
Oat Cake.   Griddle Cakes.   Maple Syrup.

HOURS FOR MEALS

Breakfast from 7.30 to 10.30 o'clock.   Late Dinner from 6.00 to 7.00
Luncheon from 12.30 to 2.30   Sunday Dinner, 2.00 only.
Dinner from - 1.00 to 2.30   Tea from - - 7.00 to 10.30

CHILDREN AND SERVANTS.

Breakfast, 7.00 o'clock.   Dinner, 1.00 o'clock.   Tea, 6.00 o'clock

NOTICE

An extra charge will be made for any dishes ordered that are not designated on this Bill,
and also for meals sent to rooms.
Guests will observe that, to secure a Warm Breakfast, a little time is required for Cooking
after the order is given; hence this notice for seeming delay.

JOHN IMRIE, Printer, 28 Colborne Street,

A breakfast menu from 'The Queen's Royal.'

Food to Fortify

Let's hope the Royal party slept in the following morning! A breakfast such as the one opposite would certainly help make amends after an excessively wearying night.

On the menu under "Miscellaneous" you will notice "Corn Bread." This recipe for corn bread, and the following one, for fruit cake, were found in one of the hotel's old handwritten ledgers, dating to the 1860s.

CORN BREAD*

[Sour milk (not the same as sour cream) cannot be bought in our hygienic culture. However it was always to hand in pre-refrigeration days and was used in conjunction with baking soda (bicarbonate of soda) as a leavening agent. Baking completely kills the harmful bacteria. If you cannot bear the idea of letting milk "go off" by sitting it in a warm place for 24 hours, try curdling it with 1 T.vinegar to 1 c. milk.]

2 c. sour milk
1 c. milk
1 T. butter, melted, cooled
1 c. flour
2 c. Indian meal [cornmeal]
1 T. sugar   1 t. soda   pinch salt

Heat oven to 400°F. Mix sour milk, fresh milk and butter. Combine flour, cornmeal, sugar, soda and salt. Stir milk mixture into meal mixture till combined. Pour into 9x5x2 inch loaf pans. Bake till golden, 35-40 mins. Cool in pans 5 mins. Turn out onto rack and finish cooling. Makes 2 loaves.

LEMON FRUIT CAKE*

$^1/_2$ c. butter
1 $^1/_4$ c. sugar
3 small eggs
1 $^3/_4$ c. flour
$^1/_2$ lemon, juice and grated rind
$^1/_3$ c. sour milk
$^2/_3$ c. raisins
$^2/_3$ c. currants
a little sliced citron

Switch oven to 350°F. Lightly flour the fruit. Grease and line 9x5x3 inch loaf pan with paper. Grease paper. Cream butter and sugar. Beating steadily, add eggs, singly. Then add flour alternately with lemon juice and rind; next the sour milk, and lastly floured fruit. Combine well. Spread evenly in pan. Bake 50-75 mins, or until tester comes clean. Cool in pan on rack 20-30 mins.

Captain Retallack, Lady Head, wife of the Governor General (r. of centre), Colonel Bradford and others on the lawn of Government House, Toronto, 1858 (southwest corner of King and Simcoe, now occupied by Roy Thompson Hall).

The Fateful Painting

Until 1855 Toronto was reached by stagecoach or boat from Niagara-on-the-Lake. Since either way could be rough, the new railway made travel much more pleasant. In those days it was an easy walk from the Toronto station to Elmsley House, residence of the Governor General, Sir Edmund Head. The King and Simcoe crossroad which the residence shared with Upper Canada College, St. Andrews Church and a pub, was known as Legislation, Education, Salvation and Damnation.

This serene moment under the trees in Elmsley House's extensive grounds took place in 1858. Perhaps tea was spread on a cloth on the lawn for the charming Lady Head and her companions. But tranquil scenes are rarely as uncomplicated as they seem. At the time this photograph was taken, it was Toronto's turn to play host to the seat of government, in an endless musical chairs which every few years shunted Parliament and the entire civil service between Quebec City, Toronto, Montreal and Kingston. It was an impossible system, and a permanent capital had to be found. But whatever the choice, the wrath of local politicians and businessmen whose cities were passed over would inevitably be incurred.

In fact, the choice had been made, just months earlier. None of the four cities had been chosen, and the tall Lady Head was not uninvolved. She was a talented painter, and a sketch of hers, painted while visiting Ottawa, is said to have been shown to Queen Victoria. The sketch, in conjunction with cogent arguments put forward by her husband, is supposed to have decided the Queen. "This," Queen Victoria is reported to have said, indicating the painting, "is the place." There were many who disagreed with the choice and attacked Sir Edmund for having influenced the Queen's decision. In fact, by the time of this scene, the Heads had become intensely unpopular and remained so for the rest of their term in office.

ICED TEA A LA RUSSE

To each glass of strong tea add the juice of half a lemon. Fill up with pounded ice and sweeten.

The Home Cook Book, Toronto, 1887.

Seven very well-behaved children wait at the edge of the lawn in a Toronto garden.

Tea on the Lawn

RASPBERRY AND CURRANT TARTLETS

3 eggs (1 white, 3 yolks)
1 oz. sugar
1 oz. butter
pinch of salt
flour as needed
uncooked rice
raspberries and currants
sugar.

Make shortcrust pastry, incorporating egg yolks and whites, and sugar. Roll out to ¹/₄ inch thickness. Line patty pans and fill with rice. Bake in a hot oven till done, then remove rice. Wash raspberries and currants and remove stalks. Make syrup with the sugar and add to fruit. Fill tart cases with fruit, heat well in the oven, and serve, hot or cold. From *Ye Old Miller's Household Book*, Toronto, 1899.

LADY BALTIMORE CAKE*

[A huge, grand cake. Could be treated as two separate cakes. Its distinctive characteristic is its nut and dried fruit-filled icing.]

1 c. butter
2 c. powdered sugar
1 c. milk
whites of 6 eggs, stiffly beaten
3 c. flour
2 t. baking powder
1 t. rosewater.

Filling:
3 c. granulated sugar
¹/₂ c. water
1 c. walnut halves
6 figs
1 c. raisins
3 egg whites, stiffly beaten.

Grease and line 2 layer tins. Cream fat and sugar till light; mix in milk; gently blend in egg whites. Sift flour and baking powder twice and stir in. Blend in rosewater. Pour mixture into layer tins. Bake in 350°F oven till done, 35-50 mins. Meanwhile, finely chop dried fruit and nuts, reserving 12 half walnuts. Boil sugar and water till it "threads." Beat sugar-water, nuts, fruit and egg whites till thick. When cake cool, spread filling on cake layers. Decorate top with 12 halved walnuts.

The Magic Cookbook, Toronto, 1912.

A line-up of old soldiers of the War of 1812 on Sheriff Jarvis's lawn, October, 1861.

The Veterans of 1812 at "Rosedale"

On October 23rd, 1861, the 5th Militia District Rifle Association gathered for a presentation of shooting prizes. It was held in the fine garden of "Rosedale," Sheriff William Botsford Jarvis's 120-acre home in the country just to the north of Bloor Street. Sheriff Jarvis was distinguished for having led a little army of farmers, mechanics and professional men up Yonge Street in 1837, easily putting to flight William Lyon Mackenzie's four hundred rebels. The gathering on the lawns was small this day as, according to the Globe's account of the event, "the weather was inclement." But General Sir William Fenwick Williams, the Nova Scotia born hero of the Crimean war, was there to help distribute the prizes. Also invited were a number of veterans of the War of 1812. At some point in the proceedings, they were lined up for a photograph. Below are a few details of some of these remarkable old gentlemen.

A Few Of Those In The Lineup:

Extreme left in uniform: Colonel Duggan. 5th from right: Joseph Dennis. United Empire Loyalist from Nova Scotia. In 1812 he owned and commanded a vessel on Lake Ontario which was captured. Prisoner-of-war for 15 months, he subsequently commanded the Princess Charlotte. 4th from right (arm in sling): William J. Woodall. Born in England, he was captured by the press gang in 1800 and forced into Naval Service. Left Service after several years as a petty officer. Emigrated to Canada, 1807, and fought at Queenston Heights. 2nd from right (with light coat): Col. David Bridgeford. Captain of 3rd Inc. Militia of Canada, he served at York, Detroit, Chippawa, Lundy's Lane and Fort Erie. He was active in Rebellion of 1837, taken prisoner and sentenced to be hanged, but liberated. Extreme right: George Ridout. Barrister, he was the second son of the Hon. Thomas Ridout, the Surveyor-General. A Lieutenant in the Corps of York Militia, he fought at Queenston Heights in 1812, and was taken prisoner at York, in 1813. His older brother, John, was killed in a duel with Sheriff Jarvis's cousin, Samuel Peters Jarvis.

The same event, showing Sheriff Jarvis's house, "Rosedale." General Williams, (or Williams Pasha as he was called, having com-
manded a Turkish regiment) towers in the centre, with sword and plumed hat. Beside him, in white top hat, is probably William

Keeping Old Soldiers From Fading Away

HOT MULLED WINE*

[In the chilly late October weather, a hot drink such as this very pleasant mull would have been very acceptable.]

To every 2 c. wine, allow
1 large c. water
1 T. sugar
$^1/_4$ t. cloves
$^1/_4$ t. cinnamon
$^1/_4$ t. nutmeg.

Tie spices in a muslin bag, add to water in an enamel pan, simmer a few minutes, then add wine.
From a loose recipe found in an 1877 Toronto cookbook.

Three months before the prize-giving, Sheriff Jarvis wrote to his daughter, Fanny, that his "most economical" new cook had put up copious amounts of strawberry and raspberry preserves. The recipes below are from an old handwritten family cookbook belonging to a member of the Jarvis family.

RASPBERRY JAM

Equal amounts raspberries and sugar.

Thoroughly heat fruit and sugar in separate fireproof dishes in oven. Then add sugar to fruit and beat till dissolved. Put up in warmed jars and seal.

WHEATEN MEAL SCONES*

[delicious scones]

$^1/_4$ lb. plain flour
$^1/_4$ lb. wholewheat flour
$^1/_2$ t. salt
1 T. sugar
$^1/_2$ t. baking soda
1 t. cream of tartar
1-2 oz. butter
$^1/_2$ c. milk

Sieve plain flour and add other dry ingredients. Lightly rub in butter and add enough milk to form a soft consistency. Roll out on a floured board to $^3/_4$" thick. Cut in 2 inch rounds and bake in 400°F oven for 12-15 minutes or until lightly browned.

At "Pinehurst" Mr. Gilbert, the art master (at left) positions the croquet ball. West side of McCaul Street, east of "The Grange,"
1864.

Bishop Strachan's Blessings

"Pinehurst" accepted young ladies for ten years until 1867 when the newly created Bishop Strachan's Church of England Ladies' School took over the building under the tutelage of the English headmistress, Mrs. Horton. Bishop Strachan's School rapidly outgrew "Pinehurst" (and, indeed, Mrs. Horton, who was dismissed within a year), and moved twice more before arriving at its present location on Lonsdale Road, where to this day it enjoys a reputation as one of Canada's most distinguished private schools.

In 1873, Madame Skelton, the school's first French and German teacher, wrote a novel, *Grace Morton*, dedicated to her pupils. In it, the heroine is sent to Madame Giatto's ("the best school in the Dominion of Canada"), a scarcely disguised B. S. S.

The education there was avant garde for a time when servants were the rule in well-to-do homes. Girls learned, in addition to art, music and academic subjects, a knowledge of domestic science, to prepare them for "the battle of life" and make them "blessings to the homes they occupy and a credit to the country," in Madame Skelton's words. One day a week, the girls prepared tea and dinner for the school. In her book, Madame Skelton lovingly paints the scene as, clad in cotton wrappers, the girls go about making cakes and apple dumplings, and preparing meat and vegetables, following sound principles of economy.

BEEF À LA BISHOP

[This recipe is adapted from one made by the pupils in the novel Grace Morton.]

1 1/2 lbs. beef (outside, round)
1 T. dripping
1 1/2 T. flour
2 c. carrots, chopped
1 c. onions, sliced
1 heaped t. parsley, chopped
1 t. savory
1 t. salt, dash pepper.

Cube meat. Heat dripping in a pan. Add meat and brown slightly both sides. Remove. Brown onions in fat. Add flour and brown also. Stir in hot water to create a sauce. Add carrots, parsley, savory, then the meat and more water if meat not covered by sauce. Cover tightly and cook in 250°F oven for 3 hours.

"Lady-like deportment" in Mr. Gilbert's painting class.

Books, Cooks & Admiring Looks

"The town is well adapted for wholesome exercise at all seasons."

Charles Dickens, *American Notes* Toronto, 1842.

And wholesome exercise at all seasons the girls of B. S. S. received, along with plenty of fresh air. In 1868, when they moved from "Pinehurst" into their new abode in the former home of Bishop John Strachan, first Bishop of Upper Canada, their walks took them along Front Street.

"When they appeared in public for their usual walk," wrote Madame Skelton, "their appearance and lady-like deportment was very striking, and many admiring glances were bestowed upon them, and followed their movements." Not least among the admiring glances following their movements were those of the young officers from the garrison on Strachan Avenue who encountered the young ladies on Front Street.

This is a recipe from the first pupil to attend B. S. S. , Flora Cummings. She had previously attended "Pinehurst," and when B. S. S. opened its doors in 1867 she arrived by mistake a day early from her home in Carrying Place, thereby becoming its first pupil! The recipe was contributed by her great-granddaughter, Robin Harmer, the fourth generation to attend the school.

MINCEMEAT CARRYING PLACE*

[Use within a week of making]

1 lb. boiled beef or tongue
1 lb. apples, peeled, cored
$^3/_4$ lb. beef suet
1 $^1/_2$ lb. currants
$^1/_2$ lb. raisins
1 nutmeg
1 lemon
$^1/_2$ lb. sugar
$^1/_4$ lb. citron peel
$^1/_4$ lb. orange peel
$^1/_4$ lb. lemon peel
$^1/_2$ oz. ground ginger
$^1/_4$ oz. allspice
$^1/_4$ oz. ground cloves
1 c. sherry & 1 c. brandy.

Chop meat, suet, fruits and lemon fine. Grind nutmeg. Combine all except sherry and brandy in heavy kettle. Bring to boil, stirring, then simmer 1 hr. stirring often. Off heat, add sherry and brandy.

A horse drawn omnibus trots past the Queen's Hotel, Front Street, 1894, where the Royal York now stands.

The Famous Queen's Hotel

The young ladies of B. S. S. must have regularly passed this way. Did any "encounters" occur as they tripped past the railings of the Queen's Hotel? The Queen's, at 78–92 Front Street, was indisputably the *ne plus ultra* of Toronto hotels from 1862 into the first decade of the twentieth century. Set in spacious grounds with croquet and tennis lawns and a glorious view of the bay, it developed a dazzling reputation for luxury and distinction. The enterprising owners, Thomas McGaw and Henry Winnett, offered their clients the ultimate in sybaritic comforts. Guests were "elevated" by lifts up to their elegant rooms which were warmed by hot air furnaces. There, in en suite bathrooms, they might bathe in hot running water and summon the servants by electric bells. It was all impossibly novel! In its day no other hotel in Toronto, possibly in the Dominion, could rival it. And its cost? In 1878 the most expensive room in the establishment would have set you back $3.50. Anything associated with the Queen's gained status. Even potted lobster!

POTTED LOBSTER (AS AT QUEEN'S HOTEL)

1 lobster
nutmeg
salt
mace
white pepper
1 or 2 cloves
butter
bay leaves.

Put into a bowl the lobster meat, keeping it as intact as possible. Split the tail and remove gut. Add the inside if not watery. Finely grind mace, nutmeg, pepper, and cloves and sprinkle over meat with the salt. Melt a thin layer of fine butter in a saucepan. Add lobster, smoothly packed, with a bay leaf or two. Pour more butter over and heat gently till cooked. When done, drain through a sieve. Lay the meat in potting-pots, selecting a variety of pieces, and surround with the seasoning. When cold, pour clarified butter over it. If highly seasoned and thickly covered with butter it will keep some time and may be eaten cold, as is, or hot, as a fricassee, with cream sauce. It looks very nice this way and tastes excellent, especially if there is spawn.

From *Ye Old Miller's Household Book*, Toronto, 1899.

'The Swedish Nightingale,' Jenny Lind, greatest soprano of the nineteenth century.

Kings At The Queen's, But Not Miss Lind

In 1886 the Queen's was at the height of its glory. Its list of distinguished guests read like an international Who's Who. They included the Russian heir-apparent, three of Queen Victoria's sons and a grandson, and President Taft and General Sherman from the United States.

Over the years practically every Governor General stayed there. Among them were the Earl and Countess of Dufferin who were virtually "hotelnapped" to the Queen's on their visit. Lady Dufferin, who had just arrived with her husband by steamer at Toronto, described in her journal how, unbeknownst to them, their Aide had engaged rooms for them at the Rossin House Hotel. However, from the wharf an informant telegraphed the Queen's of their Excellencies' arrival. Quick as a flash, one of the owners, Tom McGaw, was down at the quay and, as Lady Dufferin related, he "carried off our luggage, showed us into the Rossin House carriages and drove (us) to his rival establishment . . . where we found very comfortable rooms arranged for us." An instance of the quick wits and colossal nerve of McGaw!

In addition, the Queen's received all the chief embellishments of the nineteenth century stage — Sir Henry Irving, Ellen Terry, Sara Bernhardt, and the playwright Oscar Wilde.

Tradition has it that Jenny Lind, the "Swedish Nightingale," the greatest soprano of the era, stayed at the Queen's when she gave two concerts in 1851 at the newly built St. Lawrence Hall. But the Queen's was not in existence at the time and in fact Mademoiselle Lind stayed at Mrs. Ellah's hotel.

Doubtless prior to the singer's two Toronto appearances, Mrs. Ellah's cook prepared the special soup for her which she apparently always drank before singing, to soothe her throat and lungs.

MADEMOISELLE JENNY LIND'S SOUP

[makes one tureen]

1/4 lb. pearl sago
4 c. thick broth
2 c. cream
4 eggs, separated
8 c. beef stock boiling

Wash sago till water is clear. Add cold broth to sago in a pan. Slowly bring to boil and stew till tender. Cool. Gradually blend in the cream, then the egg yolks. Lastly, carefully stir in the boiling beef stock and serve.

From *Modern Cookery*, date unknown, missing fly leaf and end pages, found in Peterborough.

Fashionable Torontonians of La Belle Epoque arrive to attend a special event. The 'V-neck' worn by both women was considered distinctly risque when it appeared the year before.

"... Dignity And Fine Traditions," at the Queen's

Some of the guests who stayed at the Queen's had a reputation for being difficult; others merely disliked change. But whether they lived up to their reputations or how the staff coped, there is no record. For instance, did Sara Bernhardt, that role model for all later prima donnas, arrive, as she usually did, with her staff of seven and fifty trunks and insist that her bed should have five pillows, with her own fur throw and monogrammed bed linen on it? Did she order champagne for her friends and toy with "moules" herself? How did the doormen cope with the hordes of street urchins who escorted Oscar Wilde's carriage from the station, shouting "Oscar, Oscar is running Wilde," much to his delight? Could his room ever have measured up to his exacting standards of aesthetics? We do know that Mazo de la Roche was delighted with this "house of dignity and fine traditions," and the "really splendid dinner" held there in her honour when her novel *Jalna* won the *Atlantic Monthly* prize.

"Speeches by the Lieutenant Governor and other dignitaries . . . I making a small rather tremulous speech of thanks, and wearing a French evening gown, long-waisted, short-skirted in the extraordinary fashion of the day."

Did General Sherman require claret punch made just the way his wife made it? Probably not, but we include the distinguished recipe discovered, curiously, in a cookbook from Bath, Ontario.

MRS GENERAL SHERMAN'S RECIPE FOR "CLARET PUNCH"*

[This is a very pleasant punch, but distinctly sweet]

3 lemons
3 lbs. sugar
1 T. cinnamon
1/2 T. cloves, ground
2 nutmegs, grated
8 c. boiling water
1 c. rum
3 bottles claret (red Bordeaux)
3-4 oranges, sliced.

In a very large bowl peel the lemons thinly and mix rind with sugar. Add cinnamon, cloves and nutmeg. Pour on boiling water and leave for 1 hour. Add rum and claret and float orange slices on the surface.
From *Dora's Cook Book*, Bath, Ontario, 1888.

Luncheon

THE QUEEN'S
TORONTO.
McGAW & WINNETT.

SOUPS
Puree of Split Peas, Croutons
Consomme, Vermicelli

Broiled Salmon Trout, Steward Sauce

RELISHES
Chow Chow   Pearl Onions   Heinz Sweet Pickles
DRESSED LETTUCE

ENTREES
Honey Comb Tripe Sautes, Lyonnaise
Peach Fritters, Brandy Sauce

JOINTS
Prime Roast Ribs of Beef, Browned Potatoes
Boiled Leg of Mutton, Caper Sauce

VEGET-ABLES
Boiled Potatoes   Lima Beans   Mashed Potatoes
Stewed Tomatoes   Fried Sweet Potatoes

COLDS
Sugar Cured Ham   Pig's Feet   Jelly Hook
Roast Beef   Corned Beef   Pickled Lamb's Tongues
Head Cheese

SALADS
Lobster   Chicken   Mayonnaise of Salmon
LEMON SHERBET

DESSERT
Baked Deep Dish Apple Pudding, Whipped Cream
Fresh Rhubarb Pie   Boston Cream Puffs
Assorted Cake

Bananas   Florida Pines   Oranges

Walnuts   Almonds   Crown Layer Raisins

CHEESE
McLarens   Canadian Stilton

COFFEE   BUTTER MILK

MAY 23 1906

Menu

THE QUEEN'S
TORONTO.
McGAW & WINNETT.

CREAM of CHICKEN REINE, Margot
CONSOMME, Paysanne

SLICED TOMATOES

BOILED HALIBUT, a la Chambord
Pommes Navarraise

VENISON CHOPS GRILLES, Chasseur
CALF'S BRAINS BREADED, a l'Aurore
CROUTES aux FRUITS, a l'Algerienne

ROAST RIBS of BEEF, Horseradish
TURKEY with DRESSING, Cranberry Sauce
ARMOURS SUGAR CURED HAM

MASHED POTATOES   STEWED TOMATOES   GREEN PEAS
BOILED POTATOES   BAKED SWEET POTATOES
ASPARAGUS on TOAST

STEAMED JELLY ROLLY POLLY, Golden Sauce
PEACH PIE   CUSTARD PIE
LEMON WAFERS   ALMOND MACAROONS
STRAWBERRY SHORT CAKE
COFFEE ICE CREAM   ASSORTED CAKE

BANANAS   ORANGES   APPLES
FLORIDA PINEAPPLES

ALMONDS   WALNUTS   DEHESA RAISINS
Cheese-McLARENS.   CANADIAN STILTON
WATER CRACKERS   CAFE NOIR

MAY 24 1906

Two menus, one for luncheon and one for dinner, from the Queen's Hotel, May, 1906.

Cuisine At The Queen's

CONSOMME

[Both menus feature Consomme, one Paysanne and one Vermicelli.]

2 lbs. shin of beef
1 oz. ham fat
2 lbs knuckle of veal
8 c. cold water
3 cloves
3 peppercorns
1 sprig parsley
bunch herbs
1 $\frac{1}{2}$ t. salt
1 $\frac{1}{2}$ onions
$\frac{1}{2}$ carrot
$\frac{1}{2}$ turnip
1 stalk celery
2 small eggs
Rind and juice of $\frac{1}{2}$ lemon.

Cut meat and bones in small pieces. Put marrow, bones and part of the meat in large stew pan with water. Heat slowly. Finely chop vegetables and fry in ham fat or other dripping. Brown remaining meat and add to meat in pan with vegetables, herbs and spices. Simmer till meat is in rags, about 3 or more hours. Strain. When cold remove all fat. Add the whites and shells of eggs, lemon, salt and pepper. When well mixed, beat the liquid and boil 10 minutes, strain through a fine sieve and heat again to boiling. It should be of a light wine or straw colour.

Consomme Paysanne is made by adding to above a carrot, onion, leek and small piece of turnip cut into rounds the size of a quarter and cooked gently for 20 minutes in 3 c. consomme, seasoning and a pinch of sugar. Serve with a little chopped parsley. Consomme Vermicelli is created by cooking the vermicelli (pasta made in long slender threads which may be broken up) gently in the consomme for around 8 minutes.

ALMOND MACAROONS

1 lb. ground almonds
7 eggs, separated
1 lb. fruit sugar [quick dissolving]
$\frac{1}{4}$ t. almond extract.

Stiffly beat egg whites and mix well with almonds, sugar and flavouring. With a teaspoon drop on greased paper on baking sheets. Sift sugar over and bake approx. 20 mins. in a 375°F oven.

Both recipes are from *The Magic Cook Book*, Toronto, around 1912.

Child wage-earners tie on aprons and set to work, washing steps, in "The Ward."

The St. John's Ward

Quite near the Queen's hotel, but truly a world apart, was the St. John's Ward. In the later nineteenth century "The Ward" was a large Anglo-Celtic slum bounded by Queen, College, Yonge and University Streets. Where the new and old City Halls and the great hospitals and office buildings on University Avenue now rise stood narrow rows of small, shabby frame houses with decaying plaster, cluttered back yards and inadequate drains.

In 1870, the Thompsons, a large English family with ten sons, moved into number 184 Elizabeth Street, next door to the tough Elizabeth Street School. Ernest Thompson, the eighth son, small for his ten years, with eyes that tended to cross when tormented (which was often), quickly learned in his new environment to fight and use a knife. Later in life he would add Seton to his name in an effort to distance himself from his unhappy family life, and become world famous as a wild life artist and writer of animal stories. Both of the following recipes are from *The Home Cookbook*, Toronto, 1887

MUTTON AND POTATO PIE

[A form of the Irish Hunter's Pie, akin to the English Shepherd's Pie.]

6 large potatoes
3 eggs, beaten
melted butter
1 t. salt
2 lbs. mutton, cut in 1 inch pieces
breadcrumbs
salt and pepper
shallots, parsley and thyme chopped.

Boil potatoes for 22 mins till soft. Mash and rub through a sieve. Mix in eggs, butter and salt. Thickly butter a pie dish and shake breadcrumbs over its base and sides. Line with three-quarters of the potatoes, over which sprinkle seasoning and chopped herbs. Pile in the mutton, seasoning each layer well. Cover the top with the rest of the potatoes and bake in a 350°F oven for 1 1/2 to 2 hours.

SALT MACKEREL

Soak fish for a few hours in several changes of water. Tie fish loosely in a cloth, and place in a pan of cold water. Bring this to the boil, and simultaneously boil a kettle. Drain out the fish water once and substitute with kettle water. Bring just to the boil. Then take fish out and drain. On a platter, butter and pepper fish and place in oven for a few moments. Serve with sliced lemons or any nice fish sauce.

Waterworks water cart, York Street, Toronto, looking north from Adelaide Street West, 1893.

Filled to Overflowing

A crowd of adults and children fill containers from the horse-drawn Waterworks cart, pulled up on York Street, at a time when the water which supplied the street had become contaminated. It was normally drawn from the lake, but when the intake pipe sprang leaks, sewage from the harbour contaminated the water, creating very real dangers of typhoid. Before 1900 the Ward started to extend southwards, and rapidly lost its Anglo-Celtic identity as other ethnic groups moved in, attracted by inexpensive housing and proximity to the railway and several factories. There were sizable numbers of Italians, Poles and Greeks, but most were Central and Eastern European Jews, who mainly settled along Richmond and York Streets. By 1911 the Jewish population had grown to over 18, 000 and expanded to fill the area around old (then new) City Hall and Eaton's (a major employer), swelled by those fleeing the pogroms in Russia and Russian Poland.

The following recipe for Mandelbroit is from Sandra Temes, writer and authority on Jewish food. Sandra's grandparents with their tiny son, her father, were among the Russian arrivals in 1911. Her mother's family arrived later from Poland. As Sandra explained, these cookies originated from the proscription on devout Jews to eat meat and milk products in the same meal. "They contained neither, and could be eaten at the end of a dairy or meat meal. They are easy, long-lasting and relatively inexpensive — a boon to hard-working women for unexpected company, Sabbath and holiday meals."

MANDELBROIT

[Almond Bread. Traditional in Jewish homes.]

3 eggs
1 t. pure vanilla extract
1 c. almonds, coarsely chopped
1 c. sugar
3 $^1/_2$ c. all-purpose flour
1 c. vegetable oil
1 t. salt
$^1/_4$ c. sugar
3 $^1/_2$ t. baking powder
$^1/_4$ t. cinnamon.

Preheat oven to 350°F. Lightly oil jelly roll pan. In a large bowl beat eggs until frothy. Slowly add sugar, beating after each addition. Add half the oil, beat for a few seconds, then add remaining oil and vanilla. Continue to beat until well blended. Sift flour, measure, then sift again together with the salt and baking powder into a large bowl. Reserve $^1/_4$ c. and add to chopped almonds. Mix with a fork to coat nuts. With a wooden spoon stir the egg mixture into the flour until all flour is absorbed. Stir in almonds. Divide dough into 4 and shape each section into a thin roll. Place on prepared pan. Bake 20 to 25 mins. Remove from oven. Transfer to a rack and cool for 5 mins.

Slice into half inch slices. Return to pan cut-side down. Combine sugar and cinnamon. Sprinkle over slices. Bake 10 mins. Turn over and sprinkle again. Bake another 10 mins. Remove, cool on rack, and store in cookie tin. Yield: 50 to 60 slices.

Three children, of Polish, Greek and Jewish descent, play on Chestnut Street where new City Hall now stands.

Differences In Common

These high-spirited small boys race their bicycle rims happily along the Chestnut Street sidewalk in "the Ward." At home, their recently immigrated Polish, Greek, and Jewish parents might have linguistic and cultural problems, and perhaps, already, these children are aware of differences in each other's lives. But meantime, the common bonds of a sunny day, good fellowship, and how fast a bicycle rim can go spinning down the empty sidewalk, bring them together. Today, Toronto's large Polish community is concentrated around Roncesvalles Avenue to the east of High Park. Before 1911 it was chiefly centred in the Ward, with some settled between Bathurst and Spadina, slightly west of the city centre. Since no Roman Catholic churches offered services in Polish, the earliest arrivals were obliged to travel some distance across town to the overwhelmingly Irish St. Michael's Cathedral. There Eugene O'Keefe, the Papal Chamberlain, noticed this group of newcomers who were evidently having language difficulties. He bought an empty Presbyterian church on Denison Avenue, his daughter refurnished it, and they bequeathed it to the Polish community. Renamed St. Stanislaus Kostka church, it became the focal point of the Poles in the city. The recipes below and overleaf were given me by Mrs. Mary Stoklosa, who lives in the heart of today's Polish area at Roncesvalles.

POLISH BIGOS

28 oz. can sauerkraut
4 slices bacon, chopped
1 onion, chopped
1 Kielbossa sausage
1 apple, cored, peeled
1 bay leaf
salt, pepper

Boil and drain sauerkraut. Fry bacon and onion and add to sauerkraut. Add apple and cook till soft. Peel casing off sausage and slice. Add to sauerkraut with bay leaf. Bake in 350°F oven 1 hour. Season and serve. Serves 4.

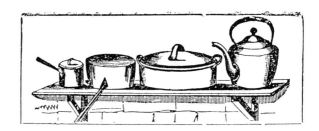

Old (then new) City Hall, seen from "the Ward." Circa 1899.

Polish Fare From Toronto Kitchens

Mary Stoklosa inherited her cooking traditions from her mother who came from Galicia in Poland. Her parents, from the town of Kielce near Warsaw, arrived in Canada separately, in 1912 and 1914, in an influx of Poles which halted with the outbreak of the First World War.

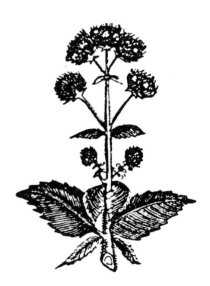

SAUERKRAUT SOUP

2 strips spareribs
3–4 qts. water
1 bay leaf
1 onion, chopped
1 carrot, cubed
potatoes and fresh tomatoes (optional)
3 T. barley
1-14 oz. can sauerkraut
1/4 lb. pork fat, cubed
1 onion, cut up
1 T. flour
1 stick celery, chopped.

Cut up spareribs. Place in large pot with water and bring to the boil. Remove any scum. Add bay leaf, carrot and celery. Simmer 1 hr. or until spareribs cooked. Separately, boil sauerkraut and drain to remove acid. Add to soup with barley. Boil gently about 30 mins. Meanwhile, in a pan, brown onion in pork fat. Blend in 1 T. flour and stir until thickened. Add some of hot soup, then return mixture to the soup, stirring well. Potatoes may be added along with the vegetables, or, in summer, peeled, chopped fresh tomatoes.

In one of Toronto's crowded schools of the 1880s a small boy closes his eyes in dread at the thought of being next under the icy scrutiny of the Visiting Health Nurse.

Health, Wealth and Mrs. McMaster

Sympathetic or not, the Health Nurses, along with the recently opened Hospital for Sick Children, caused Toronto's child mortality to plummet. The first Sick Children's Hospital, opened in 1875 in the Ward, was founded and maintained by the efforts of the enterprising Elizabeth McMaster and her band of upper class lady fund-raisers. A photograph of the time shows Mrs. McMaster, twenty-seven years old, slim, large-eyed, and with a sweet expression, wearing a nurse's uniform closely resembling the one opposite. What is not apparent is her will of unbending steel. She was the wife of Samuel McMaster, whose astute and aggressive uncle headed the Bank of Commerce and founded McMaster University. Two years after the Hospital opened in 1875, the ladies put together what they hoped would be a successful fund-raising project: *The Canadian Home Cook Book, compiled by the Ladies of Toronto and Chief Cities and Towns in Canada.* Mrs. McMaster, as Hospital Treasurer, wrote the preface. She described the Hospital's praiseworthy aims, commented on its already distinguished record, dwelt on its financial situation ("supported wholly by voluntary contribution") and ended by calling on the public to help by buying the book or contributing financial or personal assistance.

The appeal, for so worthy a cause by a group of such social distinction, was wholly irresistible. The book was hugely successful and ran into at least 80 editions, dropping "Canadian" from the title along the way, probably to increase sales south of the border.

Mrs. McMaster contributed recipes of her own to the book. Below and over are four of them.

CRANBERRY PIE

[serve cold]

4 c. cranberries
juice of $^1/_2$ lemon
$^1/_4$ lb sugar
puff or shortcrust pastry for 1 pie
icing sugar if short crust

Pick over and wash berries. Put in a dish with lemon and sugar. Cover with pastry and bake at 350°F for 45 mins. If short crust used, take from oven 5 mins earlier, cover with icing sugar, return to oven, and complete baking.

The convalescent ward in a later Hospital for Sick Children, opened 1891, on the south side of College St., between Laplante Ave. and Elizabeth Street.

Mrs. McMaster's Home Cooking

APPLE AND BREADCRUMB PUDDING

6 medium cooking apples
4-6 oz. coarse breadcrumbs
2 oz. butter
6 oz. fine sugar
$1/4$ t. nutmeg
5 fl. oz. water.

Pare and chop cooking apples. Grease a 4-cup pudding dish. Put in $1/2$ inch layer of coarse breadcrumbs. Add bits of butter over the surface. Add a layer of chopped apples with sugar and nutmeg, and repeat till dish is full. Pour the water over. Bake in 350°F oven 30 mins.

ORANGE CAKE

5 eggs
2 c. sifted cake flour
2 c. sifted sugar
$1/2$ c. water
2 t. baking powder
juice & grated rind of 2 oranges
additional sifted sugar.

Separate eggs, keeping 2 whites apart for later use. Beat 5 yolks and 3 egg whites. Gradually add flour, sugar, water and baking powder, mixing just to blend. Pour into two 8 inch ungreased layer pans and bake in 375°F oven for 30 to 40 mins.

Filling: To 2 unbeaten egg whites, add orange juice and rind and enough sifted sugar to thicken. When cake layers are baked and cool, spread this between them and return to oven 1 minute.

CORN OYSTERS

2 c. green grated corn
2 T. milk
3 eggs
2 T. butter
flour to make a batter.

Combine ingredients. Form into cakes or one large flat cake. Fry on a griddle with butter until nicely browned.

An immaculate delivery van waits on Adelaide Street East, near Jarvis Street outside his factory.
The building in the background is the old Bank of Canada building.

William Christie: bad boy who made good cookies

Once upon a time there really was a man called Christie, and he did indeed make good cookies. But that was nearly a hundred years ago. Nowadays the old Christie Brown factory, at the corner of Frederick and Adelaide Streets in Toronto, is part of George Brown College and the modern plant is in Etobicoke.

There was nothing soft-centered about William Christie. He was a clear-eyed, hard-driving, sarcastic Scot who lived between 1829 and 1900. His journal, started in 1877, gives us a good idea of the man. Business was what made Christie's heart beat and his pulse quicken. Day succeeds day with observations on the price of flour or other ingredients used in his factory. Yet, shot through the overwhelming dryness are discerning judgements about life and economics (his own and the world's in general), a flinty moral probity and a whimsical sense of humour. Periodically Christie reflects on his climb to success:

"September 3rd, 1884: 36 years today, I started to work in Toronto as a baker, with Wm. McConnell of Yonge St. . . . . I earned the large sum of $4 a month and board and lodging. After having served a 4 year apprenticeship to the baking business in Turriff, Scotland, prospects did not look bright. My hours were long. Got up at 1 a.m., was free to go to bed at 1 p.m. after having delivered the bread made by Sandy Mathers & myself per handcart. That was at the foot of a rather stiff brae. But I managed to climb up a little bittie and now have no cause to rue the day that I left my native land."

The old Christie Brown recipes no longer exist. This is from *The Magic Cook Book,* originally published around 1912 by a Toronto flour company. Although this and the following recipe have the same names as certain early Christie Brown products, they may be quite different. We have found 4 old recipes for Jumbles alone, all totally dissimilar.

JUMBLES*

[a simple, crisp sugar cookie]

2 c. sugar
1 c. butter
2 T. sour milk or buttermilk
2 eggs
1/4 t. baking soda
1 t. vanilla
flour.

Have butter, milk and eggs at room temperature. Cream butter and sugar. Add eggs, vanilla and some of flour. Dissolve the soda in milk and add to mixture. Add sufficient flour to make a dough just stiff enough to roll out thinly. Cut in circles and bake in 350°F oven for 18 to 20 mins.

Boxes of William Christie's cookies wait on dockside prior to being put aboard a schooner at Killington, Quebec. It is believed that they were part of the supplies being assembled by a doctor who was headed north to work among the Inuit.

The Crusty Fellow

Christie recalled in his 1893 journal his four year baking apprenticeship in Scotland.

"My pay was to be one pound sterling per year and a pair of boots if I was a good boy. I didn't get the boots. I got the pound. Well that's fifty years ago. I have plenty of boots now, which would indicate that I've been a good man altho a bad boy.
"I must state the truth. I was as good a boy as I have been a man, so I don't see my right to so many boots. Fifty years baking is calculated to make a fellow crusty."

At one point in the journal Christie considers his products objectively:

"Sultanas, Bermudas, Nonsuch, Teas, English Milk, Oyster Crackers, Gem and Oatmeal biscuits. Also Arrowroot, Jumbles and Champagne. Nothing to brag about."

The following recipe is also from the *Magic Cook Book.* Christie was obviously making other things besides cookies at this time.

GRAHAM GEMS*

[Gems are little muffins, and are best eaten hot with butter and jam. A teaspoon of ginger added to the flour would make these ones more interesting.]

1 1/2 c. graham flour (not crumbs)
1/2 c. flour
1/2 c. milk
1/2 c. buttermilk
1 heaping t. baking powder
1 eggpinch salt
shortening.

Grease gem (or muffin) pans and warm. Switch oven to 350°F. Combine ingredients. Fill gem pans (or 1/2 fill muffin pans) and bake for 20 mins. Makes about 15 gems.

The outside cover of the menu for the Clan Fraser dinner, May, 1894.

Colonel Fraser's Dinner

Colonel Alexander Fraser was a compatriot of Christie's, who took great pride in his Scottish origins and links to the ancient clan of Fraser. He was city editor of the Mail and Empire, publisher, historian, and founder of the 48th Highlanders Regiment, and became Archivist of Ontario in 1903. In 1894, he helped to organise the first Clan Fraser dinner to be held in Toronto. Opposite and overleaf are pages from the dinner's menu. The traditional Haggis served half-way through the meal was prepared from a recipe provided by Colonel Fraser himself. According to the endless toast list (which would wash twentieth century diners under the table but was not unusual for its time), the guest of honour was the Chief of Clan Fraser, Lord Lovat, whose mediaeval Gaelic title, "Mac Shimi" means "son of Simon."

At the top of the menu's front page over the Fraser coat of arms are the words "Mor Fhaich," meaning "The Great Field," which is the Fraser war cry. Fraser-country place names surround the targe and crossed claymores (the Scottish shield and swords) on the back page of the menu.

The menu begins with Scotch Broth.

SCOTCH BROTH*

[An excellent broth. Neck of mutton or lamb may be found in many European or Middle Eastern butchers. Makes a tureen-full]

2 lbs. neck of mutton
1 large slice turnip
3 slices carrot
1 large onion
1 stalk celery
1/2 c. pot barley
2 t. salt
1/2 t. pepper
1 t. fresh parsley
2 T. butter
1 T. flour.

Dice vegetables. Remove bones and fat from the meat and dice. Put in pot with the vegetables. Add barley. Cover with 4 c. water and simmer gently 2 hours, covered. Simmer bones in 2 c. water and strain this into the soup. Add seasoning. If too thin, blend butter with flour till smooth and stir into soup. Add parsley and serve.

From *The Magic Cook Book,* Toronto, 1912.

A chuirm sgaoilte ; chualas an ceol
Ard sholas a'n talla nan triath.—OISKAN.

" Smeorach Stratharaigeig ; uiseag an urlair."—SEAN-FHOCAL.

 # Menu

Soup.

Scotch Broth.

Fish.

Boiled Sea Salmon from the cruives of Lovat.
Sgadan beag Poll-a-Roid.   Pomme Natural, Anchovy Sauce.
Bread and Butter Rolled.

Entrees.

HAGGIS

PUNCH A LA ROMAIN.

Joints.

Roast Beef.   Spring Lamb.

Vegetables.

Mashed Potatoes.   Asparagus.   French Peas.

Entremets.

Fraser Pudding.
Curds and Cream.   Oat Cakes.   Assorted Fine Cakes.
Shortbread.   Cheese.   Biscuits.   Radishes.
Neapolitan Ice Cream.   Nuts.   Figs.   Dates.

FRUITS.   COFFEE.

Toast List

1. ### The Queen.
    "She wrought her people lasting good."

2. ### The Chief.
    "Tostamaid ar ceann a cinnidh ;
    Mac-Shimi mor na Morfhaich."
    " Master, go on, and I will follow thee
    To the last gasp, with truth and loyalty."
    Bagpipe Music—"Morar Sim."   *Lovat- Welcome*

3. ### The Clan.
    " I tell you a thing sickerly,
    That yon men will win or die ;
    For doubt of deid they sall not flee."
    "'N uair 'thig an cinneadh Frisealach,
    Tha fios gur daoine borb iad."
    Bagpipe Music—"Caisteal Dunaidh."

4. ### Our Guests.
    " Sir, you are very welcome to our house."
    Bagpipe Music—"Aird Mhic-Shimi."
    "Highland Fling," by Master Norman Fraser.

5. ### The Clan in Canada. *Charlie's child*
    " Kindred alike, where'er our skies may shine,
    Where'er our sight first drank the vital morn."
    Bagpipe Music—"Fhuair Mac-Shimi air ais an Oighearachd."

6. ### Distinguished Clansmen.
    " Of singular integrity and learning,
    Yea, the elect o' the land."
    (a) In Art ; (b) in Science ; (c) in Literature ;
    (d) in Theology ; (e) in War ; (f) in Political Life.

7. ### The Ladies.
    " Disguise our bondage as we will,
    'Tis woman, woman, rules us still."
    " And when a lady's in the case,
    You know, all other things give place."

8. ### Deoch an Doruis.
    Air (fonn) " Clementine."
    Deoch an doruis, deoch an doruis,
    Deoch an doruis, 's i tha ann ;
    Deoch an doruis, sguab as i,
    Cha'n eil Mac-na-Bracha gann.

Auld Lang Syne.   **God Save the Queen.**

The bagpipe music will be furnished by Mr. Robert Ireland, Pipe Major of the
48th Highlanders, Toronto.

The inside of the menu for the Clan Fraser dinner, with Col. Fraser's written comments.

The Queen, The Chief, The Clan

COLONEL FRASER'S GENUINE SCOTCH HAGGIS

[It is most improbable that Colonel Fraser ever actually made a haggis himself, although he plainly knew how it was prepared. The instructions are accurate. There is, however, something just a little grisly about this recipe. Was Fraser in fact having fun in perpetuating the myth of the dreaded Haggis among the Sassenachs? (Sassenach, a pejorative word originally meaning Saxon, came to mean all non-Scots.)]

Clean a fat sheep's pluck [the heart, liver and lungs] thoroughly. Make [an] incision in the heart and liver to allow the blood to flow out, then parboil the whole, letting the windpipe lie over the side of the pot to permit the phlegm and blood [to] disgorge from the lungs. The lights [lungs] cannot be overboiled but half an hour boiling does for the rest. Throw back half the liver to boil till, when cold, it grates easily. Take the heart, half the liver and parts of the lights, trimming away all skins and black-looking parts, then mince them very fine. Mince 1 lb. good beef suet, grate the half liver, and add 4 onions, peeled, scalded and minced. Mix all together. Add a large cup finely ground oatmeal, toasted till light and perfectly dry. Season with pepper, salt and a little cayenne. Take a perfectly clean [use washing soda & boiling water; it should be white] Haggis bag (sheep's stomach). See it has no thin parts in it as it may burst. Put in the meat and 1 cup good beef gravy. Do not fill too full to allow room for the meat to swell. Sew up the bag and when it swells in the pot, prick with a long needle. Then boil slowly for 3 hours.

(And there ye are.)

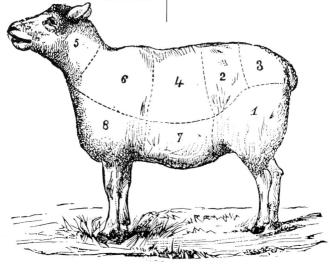

Sheep's heid kail,— a soup of kail – cabbage in which a sheep's head is boiled.
Kail is a generic word for cabbages, but, in Scotland the variety known as "Curly green", which grows tall and furnishes the "kail runts", is that usually made into "kail" broth. —

Curds and Cream,— Curds are made of sweet milk curdled by rennet. ~~and~~ taken with cream while warm and without separating the whey.

Fraser's written descriptions of various Scottish dishes (his 'curds' are not drained of their whey).

Highland Puddings

"Fraser Pudding," listed on the menu under Entremets, contains strawberries, as strawberry flowers are one of the motifs on the ancient Fraser arms and arose from a pun in Old French on the Fraser name ("freze," meaning strawberry). The pudding also customarily contains red currants. In fact, according to Colonel Fraser's daughter, it is a form of Summer Pudding, consisting of alternating layers of gently stewed whole fruit and slices of trimmed white bread soaked in the stewed juice. A weighted plate is laid on top and the dish chilled till it forms a kind of cake. It is then eaten with cream, or as here, "Curds and Cream."

CURDS AND CREAM

[Berries of all kinds are excellent served with "Curds and Cream," a very old dish which has its origins in the Scottish Highlands. There it is sometimes known as Hatted Kit and on occasion mixed with malt whiskey and lemon, and served with oatcakes. Rennet is used in cheese-making to curdle the milk. Today's rennet is much purer and stronger than the old rennet, so you will need barely any. Rennet may be found in a few health food stores. If in tablet form, powder it.]

6 c. milk
1 1/2 t. rennet
1 c. whipping cream
powdered sugar and nutmeg to taste.

Warm milk to blood heat. Off heat, add rennet. Pour into a bowl and leave overnight. When it has become curd, tie loosely in a thin cloth and hang to drain (do not wring or press the cloth). When drained, put the curd into a bowl and chill. To serve: gently remove any whey which may have re-accumulated. Lay curd in a deep dish and pour cream over it. Eat with powdered sugar and grated nutmeg, if wished.

From *The Canadian Family Cook Book*, Toronto, 1914.

King Street East, between Yonge and Church Streets, south side, 1895.

Top Shops & High Risers

"The shops (are) excellent. Many of them have a display of goods in their windows such as may be seen in thriving county towns in England, and there are some which would do no discredit to the metropolis itself."
—— Charles Dickens, *American Notes,* Toronto, 1842.

Coachmen and horses wait patiently along an elegant stretch of King Street. At the "Golden Lion" (left, with high-arched windows), gentlemen purchased shining top hats or fine cloth capes. Murray's drew the ladies with the latest trends. On the right, Nordheimer's offered concert tickets, sheet music or a new Steinway to gladden the heart of one's children's music master, if not the children.

A Bavarian who combined musical gifts, charm, and business acumen with telling flair, Samuel Nordheimer arrived in North America to seek his fortune at the age of fourteen. When nearly fifty, he married Edith Louisa Boulton, connected with the prominent family which owned "The Grange," the handsome house behind the Art Gallery of Ontario.

"Glenedyth," called after his young wife, was the name of Nordheimer's own palatial home, built on an eastern spur of Davenport hill and soon upstaged by the colossal Casa Loma put up by his neighbour, Sir Henry Pellatt.

In Glenedyth's tower room Nordheimer kept a telescope to survey the extensive view. Perhaps it was also used on occasion to track down any of his eleven children who might have gone astray.

Christmas at Glenedyth must have been an event of enormous excitement and anticipation. For Mrs. Nordheimer, one of *the* hostesses of her day, it must have resembled commanding the fleet on manoeuvres. One pictures a giant Christmas tree aglow with candles in the German tradition, the huge house bustling with servants polishing, dusting, whisking sheets out of cupboards and onto guest beds and excited children out of bathtubs and into party clothes. In the kitchen the real protagonist of the day, the cook, circulates among her pots. The butler uncorked the bottles for her pudding well before breakfast. Now its steam bedews the window for it has boiled since nine in the morning to be ready for dinner. What a pudding it will be!

"Glenedyth"

Christmas at Glenedyth

GLENEDYTH CHRISTMAS PUDDING (for 16)

[Mrs. Nordheimer donated this recipe for Christmas pudding to a cookbook of the time. It may sound immense but would have been insufficient for her own family and servants.]

1 1/2 lbs breadcrumbs
1/2 lb. flour
2 lbs. chopped suet
2 lbs. raisins, chopped
2 lbs. currants
2 lbs. sugar
2 oz. sliced almonds
2 oz. candied peel
2 oz. citron (or lemon peel)
2 oz. preserved ginger
2 small nutmegs, grated
2 limes, rind and juice
1 t. salt
18 eggs, beaten
5 fl. oz. brandy
3 to 4 fl. oz maraschino.

Finely chop ginger. Combine all ingredients except last three; stir in eggs and if mixture needs more moistening, add a little milk to the egg mixture, but be careful as milk will make the pudding heavy. Add brandy and liqueur last. Put in a floured cloth and tie loosely. Boil 10 hrs, in a large kettle, keeping the water level 3/4 full and the temperature at boiling.

SAUCE

10 egg yolks
4 oz. sugar
2 c. milk
1 1/2 c. Madeira

Stir in a double boiler until a rich custard has formed. Add Madeira. Strain and serve hot.
The Canadian Family Cook Book, Toronto, 1914.

A garden party at the Grange.

A Garden Party at the Grange

It had been a very long hot day. That evening, despite his weariness, and before returning to Mrs. Chin and the eleven little Chin children in the lodge beside the gates, Mr. Chin the butler made his daily entry in the pages of his pantry book.

He wrote under the column entitled "Remarks etc,"

"Monday, 23rd August, 1897,
Governor General and Lady Aberdeen present Pd. Mr.
Collins for waiting [at] Garden Party.
Miss Crookshanks 5 dozen eggs pd."

The garden party was given by his employers, Professor and Mrs. Goldwin Smith, at their home, The Grange (". . . a lovely place — quite one of the oldest houses in Toronto with beautiful grounds," Lady Aberdeen reminisced in her journal two weeks later).

It was in honour of the visiting British Association for the Advancement of Science, whose arrival had triggered a perfect flurry of social activity in Toronto's usually sleepy month of August. Furthermore, Lord and Lady Aberdeen, who had arrived from Ottawa in their role as patrons of the British Association (or "British Ass.," as Lady Aberdeen would abbreviate it in her journal) had been invited by the Smiths. The fact that Professor Smith was very well known as a republican and advocate of union with the United States, and that he deplored the existence of a vice-regal court in Canada, was not for one minute lost upon the Aberdeens. Thus Lady Aberdeen, incredulity springing her pen strokes, wrote:

"Yes, the Goldwin Smiths! Who would have thought that the day would come when H. E. & Goldwin Smith would have been seen hobnobbing together, & H. E. drinking his host's health in a silver gobblet [sic] belonging to the first Governor of Ontario. It is a curious fact that [Goldwin Smith]. . . . should also be the man to receive us in the most absolute royal manner, every point of etiquette being most formally observed — special gate reserved for our carriage alone to enter, band ready to strike up . . . red cloth — the Goldwin Smiths themselves on doorsteps & hat in hand . . . ready to fetch anyone we wanted to speak to. It was all very funny."

From *Canadian Journal of Lady Aberdeen, 1893-98.*
edited with an introduction by John Saywell.
Toronto, The Champlain Society.

The formidable Mrs. Goldwin Smith in the Garden of the Grange

Hostess With The Mostest

In addition to the 5 dozen eggs he bought fresh on the day of the party, Mr. Chin had purchased 8 dozen eggs and 11 chickens (one prays already plucked!) two days before. For the cook who, with no refrigeration, had to prepare everything immediately prior to the event, those two days can scarcely have been long enough.

What would she, in consultation with her highly capable mistress, have conjured up for a garden party tea, with 13 dozen eggs and all those birds? Tiny chicken or egg sandwiches seem too obvious, and too boring, for such an experienced hostess as Harriet Smith, particularly as she knew that four other teas offered by rival hostesses faced her guests that same warm afternoon. Instead she might have suggested this very simple chicken and egg salad which comes from the pages of her own cookbook, brought with her from her Boston home when she originally arrived in Toronto to marry her first husband, D'Arcy Boulton.

MAGNONNAISE [sic] OF FOWL

Lay in a circle, on a dish, some pieces of roast fowl; garnish the middle with hearts of lettuce; add a circle of hard-boiled eggs, cut in quarters; ornament the sides with slices of boiled carrots, some gherkins, slices of anchovy, and capers. Make a strong magnonnaise, pour it over the lettuces, and serve. Season the meat and the lettuces with oil, vinegar, pepper, and salt.

WHITE MAGNONNAISE SAUCE

Put into a bowl the yolk of an egg, pepper and salt, and a few drops of vinegar, stir and mix them well; add a spoonful of oil, drop by drop, stirring all the time. When the sauce is smooth, add some vinegar by degrees, and still keep stirring it. This is a very delicate sauce, but it requires patience to make well.

It is used to mask all sorts of cold fowl or fish. It may be made green by adding a little spinage-[sic]juice at the moment when you put in the eggs. If, in the summer, it is made in a pan placed on pounded ice, it will have a better consistency.

Both recipes from *French Domestic Cookery combining Elegance with Economy*, New York, Harper & Brothers, 1846.

The Don River, looking towards foot bridge at east end of Carlton Street, 1923.

Fish-a-plenty

Nowadays the Don Valley Parkway thunders along to the left of where these boys fish peacefully with floats and lines on the bank of the wintry Don. Was fishing in the early 1920s still what it once had been? The waters of the Don River and Toronto Harbour were once a veritable fisherman's paradise, and one of the earliest to mention it was a young woman, Elizabeth Simcoe, wife of the first Lieutenant Governor of Ontario. In early November, 1793, she wrote in her diary of a night-time fishing trip in the harbour of Toronto (or York as her husband had named it):

"At 8 this dark evening we went in a boat to see salmon speared. Large torches of white birchbark being carried in the boat, the blaze of light attracts the fish [which] the men are dexterous in spearing. The manner of destroying the fish is disagreeable, but seeing them swimming in shoals around the boat is a very pretty sight."

To prepare salmon, see p. 154. To accompany salmon, Mrs. Simcoe sometimes served an unusual sauce of wild gooseberries which she found in the meadows of the Don Valley. It is a Shetland accompaniment, usually used with mackerel or pork, and was fairly customary in the eighteenth and nineteenth centuries. Nothing of the kind was to be found in old Toronto cook books, but here is an interesting recipe from Ottawa.

GREEN GOOSEBERRY SAUCE

1 c. green gooseberries
2 T. green sorrel
small piece butter
1 oz. sugar
a little pepper, salt and nutmeg.

Wash sorrel. Press out juice through a cloth. Boil gooseberries. Drain and puree. Return pulp to saucepan and add 1 wineglass of sorrel juice, butter, sugar, seasoning and nutmeg. Serve very hot.
From *The Canadian Economist*, Ottawa, 1881.

BAKED TROUT, PICKEREL OR BLACK BASS

[The boys opposite probably caught bass, pickerel, or trout.]

8 good-sized onions, finely chopped
$1/2$ that quantity of breadcrumbs
Butter the size of an egg
lots of salt and pepper
Anchovy sauce
cayenne.

Clean fish. Mix ingredients thoroughly with enough anchovy sauce to make it quite red. Stuff fish with mixture and sprinkle remainder over the fish. Add a little cayenne. Bake in oven.
The Home Cook Book, Toronto, 1877.

Boys netting smelt.

Mrs Simcoe Goes Fishing

Later that same winter young Mrs. Simcoe noticed Indians out on the frozen waters of the bay, cutting holes in the ice through which "they were catching maskalonge, a superior kind of pike, and pickerel."

The frozen Don River, too, offered excellent fishing — "several dozen in an hour." After watching fine small red trout being pulled in, Mrs. Simcoe decided that she too must try her hand. Accordingly, she drove her carriage onto the ice at the mouth of the Don and fished out the window, "but" she wrote later in disgust "the fish are not to be caught as they were last winter." She suspected the noise of her carriage on the ice had scared them away.

Forty one years after Mrs. Simcoe's unsuccessful outing, the fishing in Toronto was still excellent. In fact Anna Jameson, authoress and wife of the Attorney General, described in her book *Winter Studies and Summer Rambles in Canada*, a winter of eating plentiful and delicious fish including "black bass and whitefish caught in holes in the ice and brought down by the Indians."

TO ADD FLAVOUR TO BROILED WHITEFISH

[An old trick that probably came to us from the Indians]

A little smoke under the fish adds flavour. This may be made by putting 2 or 3 cobs under the gridiron.

The Canadian Family Cook Book, Toronto, 1914.

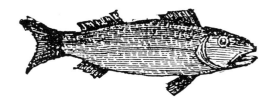

Scarborough School boys eat their lunch on the school steps, 1908.

Schoolboy Fare

In Scarborough, immediately east of Toronto, these cheerful boys attended School Section no. 7, a frame school on the north side of Old Kingston Road, west of Highland Creek. It was built in 1870 and attended by about fifty children a year until 1923, when it became a dance hall. It burned to the ground in 1951. The animal story writer, Ernest Thompson Seton, who went to school in Lindsay and Toronto in the 1860s, recalled carrying to school every day "a meat sandwich, a jam sandwich, and a hard-boiled egg."

HUNGRY BOYS' LUNCH

[A very basic filling winter dish for boys who could get home for lunch.]

> Thick slices bread
> sausages
> a little dripping
> flour
> boiling water.

Warm bread slices in oven. Well brown sausages in dripping. Stir flour into fat. Stir in enough boiling water to make a thick, rich gravy. On hot plates, arrange 3 sausages on each bread slice and pour gravy over.

GINGER BEER*

[Or ginger "pop," a non-alcoholic, old fashioned drink much enjoyed by children and adults. Combined with beer it makes the authentic "shandy."]

> 5 c. boiling water
> 6 oz. fine sugar
> 1 oz. fresh ginger, bruised
> 1 oz. cream of tartar
> 3/4 lemon, juice and rind
> 3/4 t. brewers yeast.

Pour boiling water onto all ingredients except yeast. Stir well. When lukewarm, add yeast. Cover and let stand 2 days in warm place. Strain, bottle and cork.

Both these recipes are from *The Canadian Home Cook Book*, Toronto, 1914.

Barnraising in Markham area. Arthur Reesor barn.

Plain Folk From Pennsylvania

In the townships of Richmond Hill and Markham near Toronto are many farmers of German or Swiss origin who have cultivated their land for nearly two centuries. The Reesor family are Mennonites who settled in Markham Township in 1804. They originated in Switzerland, but were exiled in the early 1600s to the German Palatinate because of their religious beliefs. About a hundred years later, they arrived in Lancaster County, Pennsylvania, seeking fertile land and a sympathetic environment in which to practise their quiet, peaceful beliefs. After the American Revolutionary war, the inexpensive land offered by the British Government attracted many Mennonites to Upper Canada (Ontario), and most who came settled around Waterloo County.

The Reesors, too, made the difficult journey northwards, travelling in Conestoga wagons, but they continued further east and arrived in the area of what is now Markham. Initially Joseph Reesor called the tiny settlement Reesorville, after his family, but finally adopted the name of Markham, which Lieutenant Governor Simcoe had given the Township about ten years before. Today, one of Joseph's many descendants, Murray Reesor, lives near Markham in the fine old farm that has belonged to several generations of the family.

Mennonite fashion, it consists of two completely self-contained units. The larger, which was the original farmhouse, is now occupied by Murray's eldest son and his family, and the smaller, which Murray built on for his parents when he was young, houses himself and his wife Dorothy. This is known as the "doddy" house, from "gross doddy," meaning grandfather in Mennonite German.

Dorothy and Murray still speak this German dialect to each other (although their children do not), and regularly attend the Mennonite church near their farm. They are typical of progressive Mennonites, the majority of today's Mennonites, in that their dress, though quiet, is not distinctive and they feel free to drive automobiles, as opposed to horse-drawn vehicles. Inside and out, the Reesor farm manifests endless daily care; in its buildings, fine animals and implements; in the handsome poultry which scratch in the yard; and the kitchen, with its thriving plants, confident cat and smells of baking. All has an orderly simplicity expressive of a religion which, besides its deep spiritual values, finds beauty in down-to-earth, practical things. These recipes are from handwritten books which have been handed down through the family to the gentle and charming Dorothy Reesor.

Farm children collect eggs in a hat.

The Markham Mennonites

YANKEE PENNSYLVANIA PIES (makes 4 pies)

1 c. sugar
2 c. flour
$1/2$ c. syrup
$1/2$ c. lard
2 c. water
1 c. brown sugar
1 T. flour
1 t. soda
1 t. cream of tartar
1 egg
1 t. vanilla

crumbs.

Mix first six ingredients together. Boil 1 minute till thick. Make crumbs by rubbing lard into the mixed dry ingredients. Pour syrup mix into uncooked pastry shells; top with crumbs. Bake in a 410°F oven for 10 mins., reduce heat to 350°F and continue baking 20 minutes.

AUNT FANNY'S OATMEAL COOKIES

[Both the following are easy and excellent]

3 c. oatmeal
2 c. flour
2 c. brown sugar
1 c. raisins, chopped fine
1 t. cinnamon
1 c. melted butter
2 eggs, beaten
1 t. bicarb. soda
5 t. sour milk.

Mix together dry ingredients. Add melted butter, eggs, soda and sour milk. Drop by teaspoonsful onto greased cookie sheet. Bake at 375°F for 10 to 12 mins. Cool on sheet. Makes about 60 cookies.

MOTHER REESOR'S BROWNIES (circa 1922)

$1/2$ c. melted butter
1 c. sugar
2 T. cocoa
1 c. walnuts
$1/2$ c. flour
2 eggs, beaten
1 t. vanilla
1 t. baking powder.

Combine ingredients. Spread in a 9x9x2 inch square pan. Bake in a 350°F oven for 25 to 30 mins. Before this cools, cut in squares.

Lucy Maud Montgomery (in large black hat) with Red Cross Workers, circa 1915.

Lucy Maud Montgomery in Ontario

Lucy Maud Montgomery, author of *Anne of Green Gables* and many other books, wrote frequently about the province of her birth, Prince Edward Island. But she lived nearly half her life in Ontario, about fifty miles northeast of Toronto. Maud (as she was known) was born in 1874 at Clifton, P. E. I. , and after her mother's death, was raised on her grandparents' farm at Cavendish. At an early age she began to write and later worked as a newspaper reporter, author and teacher. At 37 she married a Presbyterian minister, Ewen Macdonald, and moved to Ontario when he became the incumbent of the Presbyterian Church in the village of Leaskdale. However, neither marriage, motherhood, nor her role as minister's wife checked the flow of Maud's writing. In fact, her thoughts constantly revolved around it. For a time the Macdonalds employed a young Leaskdale girl, Ellen Bushby, to help them in the Manse.

Now a spry old lady in her eighties, she remembers the minister's wife as a "warmhearted, very bright woman." Yet it must have seemed an exceedingly strange household to the young girl. A photograph of the Manse in Molly Gillen's biography of L. M. Montgomery shows an interior of Ibsenesque gloom.

Of Mr. and Mrs. Macdonald, Ellen commented, "A very odd couple the two of them. As queer as ducks. She was always going around whispering to herself, sometimes loud enough to be understood." Macdonald, too, was irritable, and "given to strange fits of melancholy when he simply sat staring blankly before him." In fact, although young Ellen thought him simply "very odd" the unfortunate Macdonald was suffering from severe manic-depression. Ellen remembers Maud routinely writing "from 9 till midday every day." Her success must have done much to supplement a country minister's income, and enabled her to escape the reality of his worsening condition. In 1926 the Macdonalds moved from Leaskdale to Norval, a village west of Toronto. Ellen went too, but the isolation was too much and she returned home. The Macdonalds remained there nine years, during which poor Maud's own health suffered severely as she struggled to continue as if all were well. On Ewen's retirement they moved to a large house called "Journey's End" on Riverside Drive in the Humber area of Toronto where Maud wrote her last three novels. *Anne of Ingleside*, published in 1939, was her last. She died in 1942, followed two years later by her husband.

Leaskdale Manse in winter.

Meals at the Manse

Ellen Bushby (or Davidson as she is now) recalled that at New Year, while she worked at the Manse, a pork roast was baked in a thick crust of flour and water and the crust discarded after the roast was cooked. She also recalled that every Christmas a box of dried salt cod would arrive from Prince Edward Island. This was soaked overnight, boiled for 30 minutes or so, and served with plain, boiled potatoes and pickled beets. With telling frugality, leftovers were formed into cakes, egg-dipped and fried. Following are two of Maud's recipes which Ellen baked for the family. ("Aunt Annie" was Annie Campbell, a favourite maternal aunt of Maud's).

AUNT ANNIE'S LEMON PIE

2 eggs, separated
pinch salt
pastry for 1 t. butter
1 c. sugar
1 lemon, rind and juice
2 T. flour
1 c. milk
1 pie shell

Mix egg yolks and next five ingredients. Add milk and stir well. Line pie plate with pastry. Beat egg whites stiff and fold onto mixture. Bake in 350°F oven for 40 minutes, taking care not to let burn.

DATE LOAF*

[a very pleasant cake bread]

1 c. dates, chopped
1 t. bicarb. of soda
1 c. boiling water
1 c. brown sugar
1 c. (or more) flour
$1/2$ t. salt
2 oz. butter
1 egg
1 t. vanilla.

Pour boiling water over dates and soda. Let stand a few minutes. Add rest of ingredients, mixing thoroughly. Bake in 350°F oven about 1 hour.

Opposite is a challenging flight of steps, at Port Hope, about six miles from Cobourg.

Mrs. Stewart's Cook Has a Fall

Almost 100 years before Lucy Maud Montgomery, another literary wife had much to endure when her husband fell ill in Cobourg, a small town in the centre of Lake Ontario's northern shore. In 1822 Frances Stewart and her husband Thomas sailed from Belfast with their children and three servants for a life in the "far-off backwoods of Canada." Thomas had been a wealthy manufacturer but had suffered major reversals. In spite of this, and the fact that he suffered from a severe limp, he was an agreeable and energetic man. Frances herself "had been brought up in all the refinements of high cultivation." She wrote many letters to several close friends back home, which were compiled into a book, *Our Forest Home*. It forms a fascinating record of the Stewarts' new life, spent in the area of Peterborough (which was, in fact, named at Frances' suggestion after their friend Peter Robinson, who settled 416 Irish families around there. Its original name was Scott's Mills). Both the Stewarts and their in-laws, the Reids, who accompanied them to Canada, had been granted extensive land in Douro Township near Peterborough. Before they got there, Mr. Stewart became ill in Cobourg. To make matters worse, the Stewarts' cook fell on icy steps carrying a tub of water and broke several ribs, so Frances, who had never cooked in her life before, had to produce all the meals for her own and her in-laws' families and servants. To do this she "was obliged to refer to her cookery book for directions," a book which she plainly brought with her. *The Stewart Cookbook*, written in 1782 in an exquisite hand (too early to be her own), was found among Mrs. Stewart's belongings after her death, and may very possibly have been the one to which she referred in 1822.

SACK POSSET*

[Possets were often a sickroom drink. The base was sometimes ale but here it is sack (dry sherry). The idea of offering anything so thick and sweet to an invalid seems strange. However this makes a very comforting drink, pleasant to sup with a spoon, but definitely not designed to quench feverish thirsts!]

1 c. cream
$^1/_2$ t. powdered mace
2 eggs, separated
1 or more t. sugar
$^1/_4$ c. dry sherry
1 or more t. sugar.

Beat yolks with $^1/_2$ an egg white. Heat cream in a pan. Add mace. Mix most of egg mixture with cream taking care it doesn't curdle. Sweeten to taste. Heat a double boiler to boiling. Off heat, add sherry and remaining egg whites to upper pan. Sweeten this and mix well. Put upper pot on the boiling water, combine cream and egg mixtures and stir constantly. Cover and allow to thicken. Add sugar to taste and serve. If wished, dip rim of container in which it is to be served in sugar.

An elderly servant peels potatoes in preparation for a meal.

Mrs. Stewart's Cookbook

LEMON SILLYBUBS

2 lemons, thinly pared and juiced
1 glass white wine
2 c. cream
sugar to taste.

Steep lemon peel in wine. Remove, and add cream, lemon and sugar to taste. Beat to a stiff froth. Put into glasses and leave 10 to 12 hours till fluid at the bottom is clear.

TO MAKE IRISH CATCHUP

[This recipe is as written, with a few spelling and punctuation changes to facilitate reading. It would require a very large amount of mushrooms.]

Take the largest flat mushrooms. Peel and cut the black ends of the stalks but let the stuff within remain. Mince them small in a wooden bowl and season with a large handful salt. Make it in a sort of brine. Let them stand in it three days and stir them five or six times a day. Then boil them some time, put in a hair sieve and squeeze with the back of a spoon to get all the liquor out of them. Then boil the liquor again by itself and to every quart of it put one ounce of spice, to wit, mace, cloves, allspice and pepper. Let stand till quite cold. Bottle up close. It will keep 2 or 3 years.

Guests play croquet at the home of Samuel Strickland, Lakefield, near Peterborough, 1860s.

The Literary Stricklands

One of the most attractive settlements in Upper Canada was in the "backwoods" near Peterborough, where several half pay officers and other English gentlemen had taken up land. It was very far from ideal farmland, but appealed to many, initially anyway, because of the fishing and hunting. C. R. Weed, assistant secretary of the Royal Society in England, visiting in the 1850s, felt that the society in this region had "a tone not to be found in the longer settled 'front' [Ontario lakeside] townships."

Among those domiciled there were Major Sam Strickland, author of *Twenty-seven Years in Canada West*, and, for a time, his still more talented sisters, Catharine Parr Traill and Susannah Moodie, with their husbands. Strickland lived north of Lakefield on Lake Katchawanooka, and the Traills and Moodies resided in adjacent properties. Weed describes his visit:

"On our way home, we visited some of the oldest settlers in Douro [the Township around Lakefield] who occupy very pleasant houses, commanding charming views of Clear Lake and the Otonabee [Clear Lake and the Otonabee River are linked by Lake Katchewanooka]. To those who have been educated in a school of formal conventionalities, the freedom of bush-life appears strange. Without further warning than was given by a dog, we walked into drawing rooms, the tenants of which did not seem at all disconcerted by our presence; but on the contrary, gave us a most cordial welcome, and pressed us to take refreshments. The interior of these houses is most comfortable; and were it not that the bush shuts out the distant view, it would require no great effort to imagine the scenery English."

From *Lumbering and Farming near Peterborough*, included in *Early Travellers in the Canadas*.

CATHARINE PARR TRAILL'S "EXCELLENT HOT TEA CAKES"

2 c. flour
1 oz. butter, softened
1 t. cream of tartar
1/2 t. baking soda
milk to mix.

Grease baking sheet. Sift flour, cream of tartar and soda. Rub in butter with fingertips. Mix with milk to form a soft dough. Roll to 1 inch thickness. Cut out with a tumbler. Bake at 400°F for 20 to 25 mins. Serve hot.

From Catharine Parr Traill's *The Canadian Settler's Guide.*

Participants in a barn-raising bee are served a fine meal by several young women. 1909.

Bees & Sprees

"Bees" were called to carry out tasks which settlers could not readily accomplish alone, such as putting up a barn or house, logging or stumping land, or processing large amounts of food or material. In return for the help, the settler's wife provided a feast, or "spree," for the workers, which could involve her and other neighbourhood women in extremely hard work for several days beforehand. This was the only reward expected by the workers, but the isolated young male settlers probably always looked forward to the fun and flirting that often came along with the food. Frances and Thomas Stewart, the early pioneers of Douro, called a bee in 1841 to put up their new home. Eighteen neighbours responded including young women who helped Mrs. Stewart prepare such a noble feast that her workers could scarcely be got rid of! After a morning's work, the builders sat down to a roast pig, fish, a boiled leg of mutton, and a large cold mutton pie, with mashed potatoes, beans, and carrots. This was followed by pies and cakes, a large rice pudding, a large bread and butter pudding, and currant and gooseberry tarts. The work continued afterwards but rain stopped the proceedings, whereupon the men went into the old house and drank punch and smoked cigars, while much chatting and flirting took place among the young people. Later, there was a substantial tea, followed by dancing and fiddling till 1 a. m., with a late night supper almost as large as the dinner. With such a whale of a time in progress, the rain provided an excellent excuse for all to have to be put up overnight! However, in the morning all were working hard again before breakfast and by noon the house was up.

The Stewarts were close friends of the rather younger Catherine Parr Traill and her husband .

CATHARINE PARR TRAILL'S
WILD RICE PUDDING*

[This makes a very agreeable dessert. Wild rice was harvested in nearby Rice Lake.]

Carefully wash 1 c. Indian rice. Soak for several hours, changing the water twice. Drain. Put in a saucepan with 2 1/2 c. water, cover pan and boil for 30 minutes. Drain. Substitute milk for water, adding a pinch of salt, and barely simmer for about 1 hour or till milk is absorbed and every grain burst. Cool, then add 4 beaten eggs, 1 1/2 oz. butter and 3 oz. sugar. Sprinkle over a little nutmeg or cinnamon. This makes an excellent baked or boiled pudding. [A good handful of raisins would make a nice addition too.]

From *The Canadian Settler's Guide.*

A small team of workers puts up the framework of a barn in the Ontario countryside.

Honey For The Bees

In their turn Thomas and Catharine Parr Traill called a bee to build their first house in the bush, near Lakefield. Two years later, Mrs. Traill's sister, Susannah Moodie, and her husband held a logging bee. Mrs. Moodie, a less sanguine soul than her sister, anticipated trouble. Logging Bees, she commented darkly, "are noisy, riotous, drunken meetings, often terminating in violent quarrels, sometimes even in blood shed." After the event, she recounted that "thirty two men, gentle and simple, were invited to our bee," but then made manifestly clear that she didn't find many of them the least gentle or simple! Disapproval notwithstanding, for the occasion she and her maid served pea soup, legs of pork, venison, eel, plenty of potatoes, raspberry pies, and to drink, a large kettle of tea and the inevitable whiskey ("the honey," as her sister Catharine put it, "that our *bees* are solaced with.").

Catharine Parr Traill felt "the black raspberry makes the best pie . . . as it is sweeter and richer." She also suggested removing the prickles from the berries of wild gooseberries by soaking them in boiling water for a minute and rubbing off the prickles with a clean coarse cloth, then using the berries for pies, sweetened with maple sugar or molasses. It is interesting how frequently wild gooseberries are referred to in nineteenth century Ontario. They seem to have virtually vanished.

MRS. TRAILL'S ADVICE ON VENISON

The best joints to roast are the haunch and the loins, which last should be cut saddle fashion, viz., both loins together. If the deer be fat and in good season, the meat will need no other basting than its own fat. But if lean, lard, butter, or slices of fat bacon will be necessary. The joint should be roasted with a high heat, basted often, and sprinkled with a little salt. Do not overcook. Venison's open-grained meat loses its juice readily, and it roasts faster than any other meat.

From Catharine Parr Traill's *Canadian Settlers' Guide.*

The Parliament buildings under construction; "purity of art and manliness of conception." Timber cribs float in the river below. 1865.

Rough-Hewn Beginnings

The eye of the beholder:

"The glory of Ottawa will be — and indeed already is - the set of public buildings which is now being erected on the rock which guards the town from the river. . . . As regards purity of art and manliness of conception [it] is entitled to the very highest praise. . . . I know no site for such a set of buildings so happy as regards both beauty and grandeur."
— Anthony Trollope, *North America*, 1861.

"A subarctic lumber village transformed by royal mandate into a political cockpit,"
— Goldwin Smith, the Sage of the Grange, 1866.

". . . Ottawa, of the gray stone palaces and the St. Petersburg-like shining water frontages [had] an austere Northern dignity of outline, grouping, and perspective, aloof from the rush of traffic in the streets."
— Rudyard Kipling, 1908, in *Letters of Travel, 1892-1913*.

"This is an outrage. No one has a right to pollute the air and water, which are the common inheritance of all; we should leave them to our children as we have received them."
— Oscar Wilde, at sight of the polluted Ottawa river, quoted in the *Ottawa Daily Citizen*, May 17, 1882.

Nearly 300 kilometres west of Lakefield, beyond a stretch of pre-Cambrian terrain that cracked the hearts and backs of many a farmer, sits Ottawa, high on its bank, contemplating Quebec across the river. Anthony Trollope, briefly visiting in 1861, burbled enthusiastically over the art and aesthetics of the still unfinished government buildings. But five years later Goldwin Smith's uncharitable viewpoint was the one shared by the majority of government servants arriving in the rough, tough, thriving lumber town. In fact, for many years they complained bitterly of the stench of smoke and the unsightly piles of lumber and sawdust around the mills. Oscar Wilde, the flamboyant English playwright, in Ottawa to give a lecture, proved an unexpected ally. The sight of the river, its fish and wildlife choking in pollution, filled him with rage. His comments appear to presage the future concern for the environment.

From across the river the dignified Parliament buildings look down as lumbermen ride a crib down the Chaudiere timber slide. It by-passed the falls.

The Axe-Wielding Barons

The saw mill owners, known as the lumber barons, were hard-driving, powerful and often enormously wealthy men. Prominent among them were the Bronsons, Perleys and Booths, a tight-knit group who sometimes formed shipping or railway alliances to transport supplies up or logs down the river. Henry Franklin Bronson, an American, owned one of the earliest and largest of the mills. He and his wife, Editha, moved easily into Ottawa society and supported many charitable causes in the community. So when the Bank Street Church was devastated "by a wicked act of incendiarism" in 1881 and its Ladies' Association put together a fundraising cookbook called *The Canadian Economist*, Editha Bronson and her friends, the Perleys and Booths, all contributed to it.

MRS. H.F. BRONSON'S
RASPBERRY OR STRAWBERRY WHISK*

[a delicious sweet]

1 c. fruit, pureed
10 oz. fine sugar
juice of 1 lemon
2-3 c. cream.

Clean fruit. Combine with sugar. Add lemon juice and cream. Whisk till thick and serve in individual glass dishes.

For a time, Editha Bronson's husband, Henry, owned the Upper Ottawa Steamship Company with another American lumber baron William Perley, husband of Georgianna.

MRS. PERLEY'S CENTENNIAL CABBAGE SALAD*

[The dressing is an excellent peppery variation on mayonnaise and keeps well.]

1 cabbage

Dressing:

1 T. sugar
1 t. salt
1/4 t. cayenne
1 egg
1 t. made-up mustard
butter, size of an egg
1/2 c. vinegar.

Chop cabbage into a bowl. Combine dressing ingredients in the top of a double boiler. Stir over heat till thick. Cool, and pour over the cabbage.

J. R. Booth, and one of his sons, C. Jackson Booth, (left), with W. C. Cain, Deputy Minister of Lands and Forests, inspecting wainey (squared) timber, spring, 1925, Shirley Lake. This part of Booth's Madawaska limits is now in Algonquin Park.

Royal Chips Off The Old Block

By 1890, no saw mill in the world exceeded the production of that of John Rudolphus ("J. R.") Booth. "The king of all the kings," he was called. Yet the silent, tireless little man retained the plain ways of his dirt-poor beginnings in the Eastern Townships until his death at ninety-nine. One of the sights of Ottawa was his daily drive from his fine stone mansion on Wellington Street to the mill in his horse and buggy (although he owned several automobiles).

"His short, athletic figure, long white beard, double-breasted pea-jacket, red woollen mitts, cloth cap with ear-laps and heavy overshoes were as familiar as icicles and zero temperatures in January," wrote one Ottawa journalist.

According to the *Mail*, "he frequently drove his Dobbin to a place in the Ottawa Valley where he gave the customary dime to the hostler, who one day remarked to him that Mr. Booth, junior, never gave him less than a quarter. "He can afford to," said the king of the lumber kings. "He's better off than I am. He has a rich father." Perhaps the "better off" son was J. Frederick Booth, whose daughter married into the Danish Royal family and became Princess Erik of Denmark. A Miss Booth, very probably Gertrude, J. R.'s daughter, donated this recipe for "Election Cake" to *The Canadian Economist*, the Bank Street Church's cookbook. Ironically, her brother, Jackson Booth bought the Bank Street Church in 1912, tore it down, and put up the Jackson Building in its place.

ELECTION CAKE*

[This cake looks very pretty if red and green glacé cherries are substituted for the more conventional dried fruit.]

1 lb. sugar
$1/2$ lb. butter
7 eggs, separated
1 lb. self-raising flour
1 lb. dried fruit, dredged in flour
1 c. sour cream
1 t. bicarb. of soda.

Grease and line cake tin. Cream butter and sugar. Beat in yolks well, one at a time, with a little of the flour; then the fruit. Add sour cream, keeping back 1 T. of it, then incorporate the rest of the flour into mixture. Dissolve soda in the T. sour cream, and blend in carefully. Fold in stiffly whipped whites. Pour into cake tin. Bake at 350°F for 60 minutes.

"Earnscliff," Ottawa, circa 1891, the year of Sir John A. Macdonald's death.

Macdonald Was Late For Dinner

In 1870 a friend of Sir John A. and Lady Agnes Macdonald lent them his house, which stood about a mile or so northeast of town, on a cliff overlooking the Ottawa River. Today it is the residence of the British High Commissioner. For Lady Agnes, "Earnscliffe" was love at first sight; twelve years later, the Macdonalds bought it. The house itself, its position, and the view which stretched to the Laurentians, always delighted her. Even entertaining, hitherto something of an ordeal, began to afford her pleasure. In her diary she describes her first New Year's reception at Earnscliffe: "All the fires blazing and crackling, the house in its best order, all the servants important and in a hurry and I in my best black velveteen gown, receiving New Year's visitors. The house was thronged from noon till dinner time, with men of all ages, sorts and styles . . . the larger part lunched at a continually replenished table in the dining room and wished me and mine all the happiness of the New Year between mouthfuls of hot oyster soup or sips of sherry."

The only disappointment for Agnes in an otherwise perfect day was that, as so very, very often happened, John A. was not there.

"I had set my heart on having him with me and lo! he went away [to a council] before one single caller had rung the doorbell . . . He only came in at dinner time." But before he could enjoy any of the leftover soup and sherry, John A. was once more called away.

—— Quoted from Louise Reynold's biography,
Agnes: The Biography of Lady Macdonald.

Lady Agnes Macdonald in 1868. Food for the mind interested her more.

Eating at Earnscliffe

Earnscliffe fare is said to have been dull, which is understandable in a household with a mistress much more interested in intellectual pursuits than soups and stuffings. However, oyster soup was a traditional dish, usually served on Christmas Eve or at New Year as described on the previous page.

Dull or not, Earnscliffe food must have been wholesome. Two cows and chickens were kept to supply the kitchen with fresh produce. There is something rather appealing in the thought of the Prime Minister of Canada obtaining his milk, butter, cream, and eggs outside his own back door like many another smallholder! Did the cows ever fall off the cliff? History doesn't relate.

OYSTER SOUP

[This recipe was contributed in 1881 to the Bank Street Church's Cook Book, The Canadian Economist, *by Mrs. Thomas McKay. Agnes Macdonald would have known her well. Mrs. McKay, whose husband's uncle (founder of New Edinburgh) had built Earnscliffe, not to mention his own home, Rideau Hall, and much besides, was very interested in food, and her oyster soup would probably have been much better than Earnscliffe's!]*

1 qt. oysters
2 c. cold water
butter, size of walnut
1 t. flour
1/4 t. salt
1/4 t. pepper
1 T. mushroom ketchup
4 T. milk
2 T. cream (or more)

Pour cold water onto oysters. Put into a colander over a bowl and drain fluids into it. Pour juice into a 6 c. saucepan. Blend the butter and flour together. Mix in the salt, pepper and mushroom ketchup. Add to broth in saucepan and gently bring to a boil. Remove saucepan from heat. Add oysters, then return to heat and allow to boil up for 1 minute only. Meantime, into a well-warmed soup tureen, add the milk and cream. Add boiling broth.
Stir and serve.

All seems ready for tea in the drawing room at "Earnscliffe."

Trial by Teacup

One of Lady Agnes Macdonald's earlier forms of entertaining was by holding a "kettledrum." A kettledrum was a small version of a "drum," the fashionable name for an afternoon tea or evening party, or even one followed by the other. Presiding at her kettledrums, the fiercely self-critical Agnes tended to feel awkward and inadequate, living in terror of spilling the tea as she poured it into the cups. "I do this very untidily," she said of herself, "being, like most women who dream of stars and love scribbling, anything but neat over my tea tray."

The recipe below and those overleaf came originally from Earnscliffe. They are from an 1891 cookbook written by Lola and Edith Powell, two of the nine children of the late William Powell, Conservative Member of Parliament and Sheriff for Carleton County in John A. Macdonald's government. The girls wrote their book of recipes (some handed down within their family and others collected over the years from members of its extremely high-profile circle of acquaintance) for their newly married sister, Kathleen Sladen, and I shall refer to it as the Powell-Sladen cookbook. Lola, who wrote the lion's share, was only fifteen at the time but her handwriting suggests a poise and maturity far beyond her years. We shall see more of it. Many of the recipes had their source written after the title, including these ones.

COCOANUT CAKE EARNSCLIFFE

3 oz. butter
$^3/_4$ c. sugar
2 T. milk
1 $^1/_4$ c. flour
1 $^1/_4$ t. baking powder
3 T. cocoanut, shredded
3 eggs.

Grease and flour two 8 inch sandwich tins. Sift flour and baking powder. Cream butter and sugar. Add eggs singly, beating, then cocoanut. Add flour alternately with milk and blend. Pour into sandwich tins, slightly depressing centre. Bake in 350°F oven for approx. 24 minutes.

[This makes only the sponge, but the cake cries out for a filling. So, from another recipe in the cookbook comes this filling. Double quantities if topping wished too.]

FILLING

$^1/_2$ lb. granulated sugar
4 T. water
whites of 2 eggs
$^3/_4$ c. dessicated cocoanut.

Stiffly beat egg whites. Boil sugar in water. Pour over eggs, beating. Blend in cocoanut. Fill cake.

#46 Suet Pudding Wiggy's way. Kitchen
Suet ¼ of a lb. Flour 3 table spoonful eggs two
a little grated ginger. Mince the suet fine
and mix well with the flour. Beat up the
eggs mix with the milk and then mix all
together — well your cloth in boiling water
Flour it tie it loose put in boiling water and
and boil 1 hour and a quarter.

#47 Yorkshire Pudding under Meat
Six table spoons full of flour 3 eggs. a tea
spoonful of salt and a pint of milk — beat it
up well and take care it is not lumpy — Put
a dish under the meat and let the dripping
fall until it is hot & well greased — then pour
in the batter — when brown and set on top — turn
it. It will take near two hours.

Sauce for Wild Fowl (Mrs Talbot 45th)
A glass of Port ½ Do. Mushroom Catsup, ¼ of a Tea
spoon Cayenne Pepper. An Anchovy 3 Eschalots
chopped small, juice of ½ a lemon or an equal
quantity vinegar.

Two 2 Omelettes
Beat up 3 Eggs — Then add ¼ a pint of

Cream, some chives cut very small and a little
white pepper. Send some thick brown gravy in
the dish

2nd or Sauise of Eggs
The Yolks of six eggs, a good lump of butter
a little cream, a little salt and a dust
of sugar stirred over a quick fire & served
up on buttered toast

Dalmeny Salad Sauce
To the Yolks of 4 boiled eggs add a tea
spoonful of mustard & a little Salt 4 Table
spoonfuls of Oil, 2 vinegar, when mixed
add a little Anchovy and Harvey sauce

Sponge Cake
Take 7 Eggs, leave out 3 of the Whites, 3 quar
ters of a lb loaf sugar half a teacup full of
cold water — Whisk the eggs and sugar
for 15 minutes — Then put in ¾ lb of Flour
and twenty drops ess. of lemon and beat
it 5 minutes more it takes more than
one hour to bake.

Two "Earnscliffe" recipes from the Powell-Sladen cook book in Edith's writing. Lola's signature is below.

Recipes From Earnscliffe

"My cook is improving but I have to see after every-thing or it goes wrong . . . ."

—— Agnes Macdonald to Louisa Macdonald, 1883.

BREAD

4 c. flour
1 T. salt
pinch sugar
1 cake yeast
4 c. warm milk and water

Add salt and sugar to flour. Break cake of yeast into the warm milk and water. Pour slowly into centre of flour, stirring all the time with a wooden spoon. Leave a little of the flour unmixed. Sit in a warm place to rise overnight - cover with a blanket. Mix early in the morning. Put in pans and set it to rise again for 3 or 4 hours, then bake in a hot oven. To make buns, add butter.

VOL-AU-VENT OF EGGS

6 hard boiled eggs
butter the size of egg
1 T. flour
milk in proportion
salt and pepper to taste
Worcester sauce
puff pastry.

Chop eggs. Make a sauce with the butter, flour and milk. Season and stir in Worcester and eggs. Cool. Roll out pastry. Cut into an oval shape and shape the edges. Cut a second oval, inside the first, cutting deeply but not right through. Bake. After baking lift out centre. Pour in egg and replace the top.

ROLY POLY*

6 oz. suet
12 oz. self-raising flour, sifted
pinch of salt
jam

Mix suet, flour and salt with water to a firm, soft dough. Roll out to approx. $1/4$ inch rectangle. Spread jam almost to the edge. Roll up, sealing edges. Put in a large scalded, floured cloth, tying ends. Boil $2 1/2$ to 3 hours.

At Rideau Hall, the Mintos and staff prior to departing on a tour of Western Canada, 1900

The Sporting Governor General

The down-to-earth former soldier, Lord Minto, Governor General of Canada from 1898 to 1904, is seen here with Lady Mary his wife, seated in front of members of their staff. Between them, wearing one of his much-loved hats which somehow always looked too big, stands Arthur Sladen, private secretary to His Excellency and four subsequent governors general. Flanking Sladen are the twin columns, Arthur Guise with hat, Comptroller of the Household, and the witty, fun-loving Coldstream Guardsman, Captain Harry Graham, Aide-de-Camp. Minto, who was a passionate sportsman (he had been an extremely successful amateur jockey when young), loved nothing better than to spend entire days in the saddle or to escape for a few days shooting. Arthur Sladen, in his photograph-scrapbook, describes laconically four days on Lake Manitoba when he, Minto, and Arthur Guise, bagged 616 duck (one flinches at such carnage). Minto was also intensely fond of fishing, and Sladen's book records a week-long eastern fishing trip in June, 1900: "Four days on the Restigouche. Poor sport. H. E. [His Excellency] killed 2 salmon (21 and 25 lbs.) Self killed 2 salmon (19 and 21 lbs.). Four days immediately afterwards on the Cascapedia. Very good fishing. H. E. killed 24 salmon — the heaviest 39 lbs. and fish averaging 26 $\frac{1}{2}$ lbs. — I was fishing in Mr. Patterson's waters and killed 7 fish — the heaviest 34 lbs. and averaging over 25 lbs. each." [For many years only the Governor General could fish on the Cascapedia River, near the Bay of Chaleurs. However, by Minto's time it no longer belonged to the Government.]

SALMON

[The brief instructions below are from the handwritten Powell-Sladen cookbook. It belonged to Sladen's wife, Kathleen, and was written for her by her sisters, Lola and Edith Powell.]

Immediately on catching fish it should be thoroughly cleaned, washed, sprinkled with salt, and put on ice.

Lady Minto, on the front of a cowcatcher, gets into the act. On the Mintos' Tour of Western Canada, 29 September, 1900.

First you shoot 'em, then you cook 'em

Unfortunately, there are no recipes from Lady Minto, but here from the Powell-Sladen cookbook are some for duck and salmon.

TO BOIL SALMON

A piece of 6 lbs. should be rolled in a floured cloth, tied carefully, covered with cold water and boiled slowly for ³/₄ hour. Always put into cold water and count from the time it begins to boil. Eat with caper sauce. (Cover what remains of the salmon with a little salt and some boiling vinegar. Nice for luncheon.)

WILD DUCK

Clean duck well. Place a large lump butter and a glass of port inside. Sew up and cook in 500°F oven 18 minutes. Serve on slices of hot toast.

THE MARQUIS'S SAUCE FOR GAME

1 glass claret
1 dessert spoon catsup
1 dessert spoon lemon juice
1 small onion, minced
grated lemon rind
cayenne and mace.

Simmer a few minutes. Strain into the roast duck gravy.

The title provokes. "Which Marquis?" Rideau Hall had seen two between 1878 and 1888 — Lorne and Lansdowne. We have plumped for Lorne as being infinitely the more likely to have known about the serving of game, having fished, shot and hunted constantly over the wild Argyllshire hills near his home, Inverary Castle. He married Princess Louise, Queen Victoria's sixth child, and was a sensitive and popular governor general from 1878 to 1883.

Cricketers and spectators in front of the refreshment tents, Rideau Hall, 15 May 1901.

The Governor General Plays Cricket

"Her Excellency, the Countess of Minto invited a number of people . . . to witness the first cricket match of the season between the Rideau Hall team and an eleven composed of members of the House of Commons and Senate . . . . hearty applause greeted especially good runs. Marques [sic] were erected on the grounds, where refreshments, fruits and ices were served, and a band was in attendance."
— Newspaper announcement, 16 May, 1901.

Not quite so heartily applauding were Lola Powell and her sisters Maud and Kathleen. After all, Kathleen's husband, Arthur Sladen, was one of the Rideau Hall team which lost the day. To the occupants of Rideau Hall, with pen poised over guest list, the popular Powell "girls next door" (their home, "Edgewood," now the South African Embassy, was literally just outside the gates) were an asset on virtually every occasion. Lola especially, was a habitual guest at the endless Rideau Hall merry-go-round of sports events, parties, suppers and balls; even at small dinners for visiting Royalty and on one occasion, the young Winston Churchill.

Opposite, Lola sits third from left, in white hat and skirt, in front of Kathleen. Kathleen ("the lovely lady" as Mackenzie King called her) stands to the right of Arthur Sladen. Maud is seated at the extreme right. Lord and Lady Minto and their children occupy front centre, with Dandy, Minto's inseparable dog, at his master's foot, his mind no doubt firmly on the refreshment tents.

LEMON (OR ORANGE) WATER ICE

[For both these recipes you will need sugar syrup.] Make as follows: Add 1 lb. fine sugar to 1 c. water. Boil to 215°F (the thread), skimming. Cool, strain].

3 lemons, grated rind
1 c. lemon juice
1 1/4 c. syrup.

Combine lemon rind, juice and syrup. Strain and freeze. Leave 30 mins. or until stiff. Remove, turn into mixing bowl and beat well.

NEGUS ICE*

[A very interesting and subtle water ice, hinting, strangely, of ginger.]

1/2 bottle port (1 1/2 c.)
1/4 nutmeg, grated
zest of 1/2 lemon, rubbed off on sugar cube
2 c. water
1 c. (or more) syrup.

Combine port, nutmeg, lemon, water and syrup. Strain, freeze, and proceed as above.

Both recipes from the Powell-Sladen cookbook.

Zisboombah (alias Lola Powell), Bluebeard's favourite niece, could cook too!

Levez le rideau! (Curtain up!)

The highlight of the year at Rideau Hall was undoubtedly the presentation of the amateur play, put on in the ballroom, dubbed "The Theatre Royal" for the occasion. Any aspiring actors (and probably some who didn't aspire at all) among the Governor General's family, staff and friends were quickly dragooned into "The Theatre Royal Stock Company." It helped matters enormously that Minto's Aide-de-Camp, Harry Graham, was an extraordinarily talented amateur playwright and natural comedian who could reduce audiences to helpless mirth.

Lola Powell was soon corralled into the company. Her figure ("tall and stately," Gilbert Sladen, her nephew and Minto's godson, recalled), lazy, dark-lashed eyes, good voice and sense of fun would have made her a stage natural. In the spring of 1904 when "Bluebeard, A Musical Melo-Farce" was put on, she played Bluebeard's favourite niece, Zisboombah.

Minto thought her the star of the show. In fact, unsubstantiated gossip had it that Minto thought altogether too much of Lola. Lady Minto was away periodically and Lola was very often at Rideau Hall. Was there any more to it? Rumour always swirls about those in high places. The official presence of her brother-in-law and sister there, and so close to her own home, was probably reason enough for Lola's frequent visits, added to which she was the kind of gregarious, fun-loving creature who fitted perfectly into the light-hearted Minto firmament.

TURKISH DELIGHT*

[This unusual and very sweet delicacy was popular among Victorians. A tablespoon of chopped pistachios adds a pleasing taste and texture.]

Grease a square baking pan with butter. Set aside. Dissolve 1 oz. gelatine (or 2 pkts gelatine) in 1 c. cold water. Put into double boiler and add 1 lb. icing sugar, stirring until dissolved. Boil 15-20 mins. , stirring. Add juice of 1 lemon and 1 T. rind. Pour into baking pan. When cold, cut in squares. Roll in icing sugar. From the Powell-Sladen cookbook.

Arthur Guise and Harry Graham ham it up in the garden at Rideau Hall.

Spicy diversions

SPICED ROUND OF BEEF

Up to 10 lbs. of lean beef
1 lb. coarse brown sugar
2 oz. salt petre
$^1/_4$ oz. pounded allspice
$^1/_2$ oz. cloves
2 lbs. coarse salt.

Rub sugar into the beef and let it lie in a cool dark place for 12 hours. Then rub the salt petre, allspice and cloves over the meat and let it remain another 12 hours. Then rub in the salt. Turn daily in the pickle for 2 or 3 weeks. Then either bake in a slow oven for 2 to 3 hours or simmer for 5 hours after the water comes to the boil. A small tub is best to preserve it in. Excellent.

CAPER SAUCE

Add to 2 c. drawn butter 3 T. of capers.

RASPBERRY VINEGAR

[A popular Victorian summer drink, certainly no worse tasting and a great deal more natural than modern commercial summer drinks.]

Cover raspberries with (malt or white wine) vinegar . Let stand 10 days stirring twice daily. For every cup of strained juice add $^1/_2$ lb. sugar, and juice and rind of 3 small lemons. Boil for 20 mins. Strain. Bottle when cooled, with a piece or two of lemon peel in each bottle. Cork and seal. To use, add cold water and ice to taste.

All these recipes from the Powell-Sladen cookbook.

OTTAWA

Theatre Royal

Government House

1904

Programme

BLUEBEARD

A MUSICAL MELO-FARCE

IN TWO ACTS

(Produced for the first and last time upon any stage, under the personal direction of the Author.)

DRAMATIS PERSONÆ.

BLUEBEARD (King of Bungalore) - - - - LIEUT.-COL. DENNY

THE DUKE OF DURTISHURTZEMBURG - MR. GLADWYN MacDOUGALL
(Hereditary Governor of Rumtumfoo)

FATIMA }
ANNE } - (his Daughters) - { LADY EILEEN ELLIOT
{ MISS HORATIA SEYMOUR

CAPTAIN FRIVOLO - - - - - - - CAPTAIN H. GRAHAM
(His Master-of-the-Horse)

LÉONIE (Fatima's Maid) - - - - - - - MISS GILMOUR

MARJORIE (Anne's Maid) - - - - - MISS MURIEL BURROWES

MELACHRINAH } (Bluebeard's deceased { MRS. DENNY
RAHAT LAKHOUM } Wive's Sisters) { MLLE DE JAFFA

SIGNOR BENJAMIN TROVATO - - - - - MR. HUGH FLEMING
(Conductor of Bluebeard's private band)

DRUMMER JONES - - - - - - - LADY VIOLET ELLIOT
(Of the Governor's Foot Guards)

ZISBOOMBAH (Bluebeard's favorite Niece) - MISS LOLA POWELL

Sunbitten James, Village Idiots, }
Oldest Inhabitants, etc. - } - - - - CAPTAIN E. BELL

Crowd, Soldiery, Police, } { HON. E. ELLIOT
Pages-in-Waiting, } - - - - { MISS STELLA MAUDE
Peasantry, etc., etc. } { MR. ERIC MAUDE

MUSIC FURNISHED BY THE ORCHESTRA OF THE GOVERNOR-GENERAL'S FOOT GUARDS.

AT THE PIANO - - MR. C. J. A. BIRKETT.

The programme for 'The Theatre Royal', Government House, 1904

Two Right Royal Cakes

BLACK GINGERBREAD, 1855*

[This is a wonderful, rich, strong, spicy gingerbread in the Powell-Sladen cookbook, from the Powells' mother, Rosanna Wallis Powell.]

1 1/2 c. molasses
1/2 c. milk
5 oz. butter [or 1/3 c.]
2 t. brown sugar
2 t. ginger
2 t. cinnamon
1/2 t. ground cloves
1/2 t. salt
2 1/2 c. flour
2 t. baking powder
3/4 c. raisins
2 eggs, beaten.

In 350°F oven, warm molasses, milk, chopped butter and sugar. Stir as little as possible. Sieve together the dry ingredients. Grease and line a square or rectangular tin. Add eggs, with molasses mixture, to dry ingredients and mix well. Pour into prepared tins and bake for 3/4 to 1 hour. Have tester ready to test for dryness.

RICH FRUIT CAKE, 1808*

[A magnificent and very dense fruitcake.]

1/2 lb. butter, chopped
1/2 lb. fine sugar
5 eggs
1/2 lb. flour, sifted
1 nutmeg, grated   1/4 t. ground cloves
1/2 t. cinnamon
1 lb. raisins   1 lb. currants
4 oz. citron, chopped
2 oz. lemon peel, chopped
2 oz. orange peel, chopped
4 oz. figs, finely chopped
2/3 glass brandy   1 small lemon
1 or 2 drops almond essence.

Have ingredients at room temperature. Grate lemon, then juice it. Grease and line large round cake tin. In warm bowl cream butter and sugar till white and creamy. Gradually beat in eggs, adding 1 T. flour with each egg. Beat in spices, lemon rind and almond essence. Add lemon juice with brandy, being careful not to make mixture too wet. Switch oven to 250°F and place in it 2 water-filled trays. Work into the mixture half the flour with half the fruit, and then the remaining flour and fruit. Pour into cake pan and place in water-filled tray. Steam 5 hours, keeping trays filled with boiling water; then bake, in centre, low shelf, for 1 hour (or steam 4 hours, and bake 2 hours). Warm testing skewer before inserting. If any brandy and lemon juice remain, pour over the cake when cool.

A Kashoub homestead near Wilno, circa 1900. Notice the windmill.

The Kashoubs Settle In

Renfrew County lies to the west of the Ottawa Valley, about 100 kilometers upriver from Ottawa. Large stretches are typical Canadian Shield terrain of rugged rock where the soil affords only subsistence level farming.

The Opeongo Road connects the Ottawa River with Lake Opeongo, in what is now Algonquin Park. It was one of several roads constructed through the forests by the government of Upper Canada in an obstinate attempt to open the area to farm settlement, in spite of warnings that the impossible soil was suitable only for timber.

In September, 1859, Mr. T. P. French, agent for the settlement of the Opeongo Road, recorded in his ledger the location of fourteen men and their families on 50-acre uncleared lots along the Road. On the tenth line down, Mr. French listed "Thomas Shulest" and in the 'Remarks' column, wrote "Pole," as he had after all the men's names. In fact Shulest (or, correctly, Shulist) and the rest of the group were Kashoubs, a people closely related to Poles, whose homeland, Kashoubia (better known as Pomerania), edged the southern shores of the Baltic Sea.

It had been occupied since the end of the eighteenth century by Prussia, whose harsh measures finally drove out a third of the population. As William Makowski writes in his *The Polish People in Canada*, 25,000 arrived in this country, mainly settling in one huge group in western Renfrew. Thomas Shulist, his thirteen companions, and their families formed the vanguard of this immense exodus.

PACZKI (Mrs. Barbara Shulist)

1 pkg. yeast
1/2 c. water
1 t. sugar
1 c. melted butter
2 1/2 c. sugar
6 to 8 eggs
2 1/2 c. milk
1/2 glass brandy
1 t. salt
1 t. nutmeg
1 t. lemon juice
flour

Soak yeast in water and sugar. Add all other ingredients and enough flour to make a nice bun dough. Let rise, covered, until double in bulk. Punch down. Cover and let rise again. When doubled, roll out and cut in rounds. Let rise again. Fry in hot lard.

Grandfather Dobrowski, pipe in pocket, hands shaped by hard work, enjoys a day of rest outside his homestead. Wilno, 1911.

Along the Opeongo

The Kashoubs were to need all their faith and endurance to survive in this unforgiving terrain. Being farmers, not loggers, they were ignorant of forest-clearing. Furthermore, they had arrived too late to plant crops. Lacking English, they could not ask their Irish "neighbours" for help, who in any case deeply resented this large foreign-speaking, closed community (there would be interracial "wars" later in the century). But somehow they survived, and over the years things slowly improved. Martin Shulist, a descendant of Thomas, still lives in Wilno over 130 years after his ancestors first settled there. In fact, he observed, in his strongly accented English, "the relatives of the first fourteen families who arrived here in 1859 . . . are still around here."

In the early days, he related, the Kashoubs had to walk 50 miles to Renfrew, the nearest town, for the most basic necessities. Later, a store opened in the new mill town of Eganville, 20 miles closer. Trips to the mill with grain to be ground were combined with visits to the store. But mainly the Kashoubs tried to be self-supporting, adding game, fish and wild berries to home raised foods. After glass bottles appeared on the shelves of the Eganville store, settlers preserved their fruit for the winter, storing it in root-cellars (according to Martin, "north-facing holes dug in a hill-side"). "Apples were quartered and dried, and later in the winter they were boiled and mixed with other jams. And what a treat, yum yum! It wasn't until 1894 when the railroad was built through Wilno, crossing the Opeongo, that other items . . . could be brought in such as lemons, oranges and bananas, to change the eating habits of the pioneers."

Martin collected these recipes from descendants of the first fourteen families to settle this area.

MRS. BARBARA SHULIST'S BEET BORSCHT

4 medium beets, peeled and grated
4 1/2 c. beef broth
1 small cabbage
2 medium carrots
1 large onion
salt and pepper
3 t. lemon juice
2 c. sour cream.

Simmer beets in broth to cover for 20 minutes. Finely chop or grate all other vegetables. Add to beets and continue to simmer till tender. Add lemon juice or vinegar. Serve with a bowl of sour cream to garnish. Serves 8.

Young cattle browse in rough terrain.

Martin Shulist's Memories

"One treat that I remember as a child on the farm was when a cow had freshly calved. The first milking from that cow was very precious, and a special white cheese was made. This was served at suppertime to the whole family, celebrating the birth of the calf or calves."

At breakfast, "green tea which is still a tradition was drunk, or burnt breadcrust crumbs were boiled to make coffee."

Getting through the winter, Martin related, involved a lot of preparation. A family of eight to ten would put by one 100 pound barrel of sauerkraut and another of whole dill pickles preserved in layers of red cherry tree leaves. In addition, after the pigs were killed late in the fall, two barrels were filled with salt pork, and rings of blood sausage were made. One hundred pounds each of peas and beans were bagged, and thirty to fifty pounds of butter churned. Into the storage also went eight to ten 100–pound bags of flour (one for each family member), and forty to fifty bags of potatoes. Potatoes were used in endless ways. They were made up into delicious soups and pancakes, or, as here, dumplings, to add to stews or soups.

ANNA M. STAMPLECOSKIE'S POTATO DUMPLINGS*

$1^1/_2$ c. raw potatoes
1 c. flour
$4^1/_2$ qts. water
1 t. salt to taste
cream.

Grate potatoes finely. Squeeze dry in a clean cloth. Add flour and mix well with potatoes. Bring water to the boil and add salt. Make little balls of the flour/potato mix. Drop into the boiling water and boil for 16 minutes. At the last minute add cream. Makes about 15 dumplings.

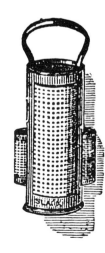

Grey owl in canoe with beaver, mid 1930s.

Madeline Remembers Grey Owl

The books of Grey Owl, describing his life with the wild animals in Canada, appeared in the first half of the twentieth century, a time when western society, increasingly mechanized and artificial, craved a link with a more natural world. They were enchanting to children and adults alike. Naturally it didn't hurt the books' popularity that the author was an intensely romantic-looking native, hawk-nosed, high-cheekboned, tall and dignified. And so literate! Then the bubble broke. Grey Owl died, and from suburban Hastings in the south of England emerged two eminently respectable spinster ladies who announced that the great Grey Owl was in fact their wayward nephew, Archie Belaney. The western world was stunned by this revelation.

Gradually the story emerged. A deeply unhappy boy, brought up in the suffocating confines of his aunts' household, young Belaney had created a dream world for himself in which he always figured as an Indian surviving in the immense Canadian wilderness.

When he was seventeen, Belaney came out to Canada, finding his way in due course to Temagami, Ontario. There he met an Indian girl, Angel Egona (this is one of several spellings of the name) of the Bear Island Band of Ojibways. Angel lived with her grandmother, her uncle, and her cousin, Alex Mathias, who was, like herself, an orphan. Belaney, captivated by Angel and the Indian way of life, visited the Egona home constantly.

I found Alex Mathias's widow, Madeline Theriault, now in her eighties, living in a retirement home in North Bay. She told me that in fact the Egona home "is where Mr. Belaney settled when he first came to Temagami. It is where he learned the Indian way of living. He also learned his Indian language from my late [first] husband's home. He was very eager to learn about Indian life. The owl wants to learn everything and turns its head back and forth, so that my uncle [in-law] said 'He looks like an owl taking in everything.' So that's where he got his name, Grey Owl. My husband took him out a lot to show him how to trap and set nets and fish, canoeing everywhere. Then they went out hunting, Grey Owl, Angel and my husband. Every time the two of them went out, my husband was told by my uncle, 'Go with them, go with them,' so he ended up the chaperone! And then they got married and shortly after they had the baby girl, and when the baby was seven months he left. He was away seven years."

Grey Owl and Gertie Bernard, or Anahareo, outside their cabin.

Grey Owl's 'Specialty'

Grey Owl returned to Bear Island, Temagami first in 1918, then after another seven-year interval, in 1925. Madeline continued her story. "When he got back (my husband and I were married then) my husband says to me 'I saw at the Hudson Bay store someone I knew a long time [ago] and I invited him over for dinner.' I said 'What's his specialty anyway?' and [my husband said] 'Boiled trout and a bannock.' The next day I cooked that special meal, and it was Belaney who turned up." When I asked her for recipes, Madeline said, "The Indians don't really have cooking recipes." (I would hear this repeatedly from other Indians). "You boil the meat or fish and drink the broth for tea. And the beef — insert a piece of stick in it and cook it on the fire." However, at a later date, Madeline wrote out her methods of preparing bannock and trout.

MADELINE'S BANNOCK*

[very easy and an excellent substitute for bread or rolls]

2 c. flour
pinch of salt
1 t. baking powder
water to mix
a little oil.

Combine flour, salt and baking powder. Use enough water to mix into a soft dough.
Knead a little. Put into a lightly greased pan. Cook it over an open fire.If in oven, put it at the back of a 400°F oven for 15 to 20 mins.

MADELINE'S BOILED TROUT

Madeline's method of preparing trout could not be simpler and consists of boiling the fish with a pinch of salt for a short time. The broth is then drunk for tea.

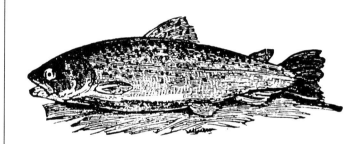

Of Grey Owl's 1925 visit to Bear Island, Madeline related, "He said then, 'I come back to my wife again and she wouldn't have me.' So not long after, he was working in Wabikon Camp and he found a friend there. Her name was Gertie Bernard. They came over to ours a couple of Sundays, both working at Wabikon, and at the end of the season they both left and I never saw him after that." Gertie Bernard, a beautiful Iroquois who became deeply involved with Grey Owl in animal conservation projects, featured prominently in his books as Anahareo.

Madeline and Alex Mathias, and their daughters, Virginia and Dorothy, 1938.

Roast Beaver With Raisins

Madeline Theriault was fifteen and looking after four younger brothers and sisters when she married Alex Mathias. "The adults arranged my marriage," she recalled. "I didn't know [him] when I married him." Life for the couple wasn't easy. Alex was a trapper and they carefully conserved the beaver on their trapline in the centuries-old Indian fashion. But suddenly licences were required to trap. To make things still harder, Alex took ill, white men moved into their area, with licences of course, and destroyed everything by poisoning the animals. These were eaten by birds and bears which in turn were poisoned. Madeline herself spoke no English until she was obliged to spend a year in hospital which forced her to learn it, and subsequently she wrote a book called *Moose to Moccasin*, sadly no longer in print. "It was very hard for me" Madeline commented, "I have no education and I was not writing in my own language."

BEAVER WITH RAISIN DOUGH

[Madeline recalls a special Christmas dinner of beaver made by her great-grandmother.]

"[She] would make dough with raisins in it and put it in the beaver as the stuffing and roast it in the oven about two hours. Tasted like dark meat on turkey legs. We ate meat all the time, it was like our bread and potatoes. Fish for a soft meal, and partridge and rabbit. Moose and deer were heavy meals."

Lucille Mackenzie, a teacher at Bear Island who put me in touch with Madeline, provided these observations on old methods of food preparation on Bear Island after talking with older members of the Bear Island Band. They are extremely basic, and everything, Lucille said, had a lot of salt pork added to it, if available, for flavour.

BEAVER

Boiled, but sometimes roasted in the oven after boiling. The stock was often reserved and a porridge made with it.

PARTRIDGE

Boiled along with a piece of salt pork, with rice, and more salt added to taste.

MOOSE

Sometimes roasted with onions; sometimes stewed, in which case the meat, along with salt pork, was fried in lard. To this potatoes were added, then water, and the stew cooked on a slow boil. The reduced stock was thickened with flour.

Dominion nickel mine and train.

Scratching in 'Trapper Country'

Sudbury is the town that came into being by chance. Sir Sandford Fleming, surveying the area for the route of the future Canadian Pacific Railway, regarded the land as lacking potential. Trapper country, constantly flooded, with minor logging.

Nevertheless, in 1883 James Worthington, the C.P.R.'s general manager, confirmed that the "unpromising" site was to become a railway terminal and named it Sudbury Junction after his wife's home in England. As construction of the line got under way, railway crews discovered copper sulphate and nickel in the rocks they were digging out. Interest in the area was galvanised! The mines which resulted eventually became part of the International Nickel Company (Inco) of New York, and Falconbridge Nickel Mines. Today they produce gold, silver, copper, cobalt, iron and more than a third of the world's nickel.

In spite of the birth of these mining giants, life in little Sudbury was singularly lacking in amenities. Sewage ran in open gutters edging the streets; drinking water came from a spring in a gravel pit; and an amateur fire brigade was kept busy dousing fires in the community of wooden homes. Not until after 1893, when it became a town, were sidewalks, piped water, and drains constructed.

There were Finns in Sudbury before 1890, working at the Copper Cliff and Victoria Mines. Anniki Maki's parents were relative latecomers, arriving in northern Ontario from Inkeroinen, near the Russian border, in 1922. The large Finnish community in Sudbury is scattered now, but as a child back then Anniki recalls hearing nearly every second person on the street speaking Finnish. Anniki is known as a great cook of Finnish food both within and without the Maki family.

ANNIKI'S MOJAKKA

[Serves 6. This very popular Finnish dish usually contains both fish and meat.]

1 1/2 lb. lean brisket
3 sliced carrots
2 onions
1 stalk celery
1 turnip (optional)
a few peppercorns
salt to taste
water to cover
up to 6 potatoes, diced.

Add water to first 7 ingredients. Simmer 1 1/2 hours. Add potatoes and cook till they soften. "The longer it cooks the better it is," says Anniki, and suggests eating it with home-made bread.

View of Sudbury looking west along Elm Street, taken from Pearl Street Hill, on east bank of Junction Creek

Dr. Howey and the 'Howling Wilderness'

When Dr. Will Howey, recently graduated from McGill, was offered the job in 1882 of providing medical care to the Canadian Pacific Railway men building the transcontinental railway in northern Ontario, he wasn't at all certain how his new bride, Florence, would react. In those days, as Florence Howey wrote much later in her book, *Pioneering on the C. P. R.*, "that part of the world was regarded as a frozen, howling wilderness, and it was too." But Florence was made of tougher stuff than most, and accept the position Will did.

After a winter in Mattawa the Howeys were moved along the line to Sudbury. She describes their arrival:

"At last we sighted Ramsay Lake [named after the locating engineer, William Ramsay; later the name was later changed to "Ramsey"] and Doctor said we were very near Sudbury . . . It began with a boarding house kept by Henry Smith [where City Hall now stands]. I remember [supper there] well . . . fried salt pork, potatoes, bread, strong butter and evaporated applesauce. It was July, 1883. There was nothing here then except a small camp and stable, built for the men and horses of an advance gang . . . for the railroad. Where 158 Elm Street East is."

The Howeys trudged up a path "between stumps and blueberry bushes," to the house built for them by the company on the hill overlooking what is now downtown Sudbury. It was named "Pill Hill" as long as they lived there and was exactly in the middle of what became Elm Street.

All my efforts failed to unearth old British-Canadian recipes in Sudbury. So I offer these which I discovered in Englehart, considerably further north. They were handwritten at the back of a 1913 cookbook found in the house of a Miss Agnes Burns after her death. It probably belonged to her mother, Mary, who, newly married, came out from Scotland and settled in Englehart at the turn of the century. Her husband, John, worked on the railroad.

BLUEBERRY PRESERVES*

6 c. berries
3 c. sugar
1 c. water.

Simmer very gently 20 minutes. Makes 6 c. preserves.

CRANBERRY CONSERVE*

[the orange makes this different]

4 c. cranberries
2 c. sugar
1 orange, unpeeled
1 c. water 6 oz. raisins.

Chop all roughly. Mix altogether. Boil till tender, 5 to 10 mins. Makes 4 c.

Principal corner of Sudbury, 1896, showing a religious procession at Ste. Anne's. This building replaced the original bricked-over Ste. Anne des Pins when it burned in 1893. The photo is slightly damaged.

The French-Canadian Invasion

Around the turn of the century large numbers of French Canadians were drawn to Sudbury. Because the railway's eastern terminus was in Montreal, Sudbury had much stronger links with Quebec than with the towns of Southern Ontario. Jesuit priests arrived early to minister to the spiritual needs of the Catholic community. On the north side of Junction Creek in McKim Township, one of them, Father Nolin, used the pines along the creek to build a log structure with chapel above and non-denominational school below. It became known as Ste. Anne's Rectory or Sainte-Anne des Pins, even after the logs were bricked over.

One of the priests had a nephew, Jean-Paul Lebelle, the thirteenth of seventeen children in a farm family near Rivière du Loup. As Jean-Paul's daughter-in-law, Margot Lebelle, observed, "only so many can inherit a farm," so around 1906 Jean-Paul decided to follow his priest-uncle to Sudbury to try his luck. Like so many others, he worked for the C. P. R. initially, then later for Inco, and finally ran his own business. But with him from his Quebec farm family Jean-Paul brought its tasty and nourishing cuisine. Margot Lebelle, an excellent cook herself, translated the following recipes for me straight from the French. Two are Jean-Paul's and one her own family's.

The Lebelle farm in Quebec kept pigs. What pork didn't get sold was made into cretons.

CRETONS

[A pork paté excellent on toast or crackers, and at Christmas. Jean-Paul's recipe was for twice this amount, which Margot insisted got used up in no time].

7 $^1/_2$ lbs. ground pork (get butcher to mince)
1 $^1/_2$ lbs. onions, minced
1 or 2 cloves garlic, or more
2 $^1/_2$ T. salt
1 T. & $^1/_2$ t. white pepper
$^1/_2$ t. cinnamon
$^1/_8$ t. ground cloves.

Cook on medium to low heat, lid off, for 6 hours, pressing out lumps. Have pots ready (sour cream containers are good). Pot up. Fat rises as it cools. Keeps about 2 weeks in refrigerator. When using, invert onto a plate.

Chalmer's Bazar and S. Johnson's store. Probably southwest corner of Durham and Cedar Streets Sudbury, 1894.

French-Canadian Traditions

On the left, Chalmer's well-stocked "bazar" seems to lack for nothing. Notice the bananas hanging at the door, the brimming baskets of fruit, and, indoors, the jars of preserves and what look remarkably like bottles of wine. At the same time, the unpaved street has raised wooden sidewalks and coal oil lamps fixed on poles.

Margot Lebelle inherited the recipe below from her Montreal-bred mother. Her parents, like Jean-Paul Lebelle, came from Quebec at the turn of the century. Her mother, Mme. Grenon, made this pate in bread pans and sold it in her grocery store. It may be mixed with mayonnaise.

PÂTÉ

4 lbs. pork liver
2 lbs. leaf lard [Order this ahead of time from the butcher. Freeze until needed.]
2 lbs. fresh pork
4 cloves garlic
4 large onions, minced
approx. 1 T. salt
approx. 1 t. white pepper
3 T. pickling spice.

Have your fresh pork ground. Tie pickling spice in muslin, or put into a tea acorn. Put leaf lard on bottom of pan. Bring all ingredients to a simmer, but cook on very low heat or the liver will stick. Cook around 4 hours, stirring. May be served as is, or passed through a blender.

TIRE BLANCHE (WHITE TOFFEE)

[Another recipe passed down from Jean-Paul Lebelle. You will need a confectioner's thermometer.]

2 c. white sugar
1 c. brown sugar
1 c. hot water
1 t. vinegar
a knob of butter.

Have a large platter in the freezer. Cook ingredients on a high heat without stirring. When mixture reaches the hard ball point on a thermometer, butter the cold platter and spread mixture onto it. Once it comes off plate, lift with cold hands and pull, as long as your hands are cold, or pass it to someone whose hands are cold. It gets very white. When ready to cut, put on buttered plate, twist and cut in $1/2$ inch pieces. Wrap. Chopped walnuts or pecans may be added.

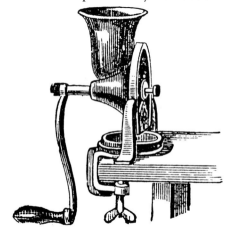

"Foam and fury." Water roars through the locks at Sault Ste. Marie after they were rammed by a ship, June, 1906.

St. Mary's Falls or Sault Ste. Marie

"The river of St. Mary is . . . . a strait [between] Lake Superior and Lake Huron. About ten miles higher up, the great ocean-lake narrows to a point; then . . . comes rushing along till it meets with a downward ledge . . . over which it throws itself in foam and fury, tearing a path for its billows through the rocks . . . ." "Here, at the foot of the rapids, the celebrated whitefish of the lakes is caught in its highest perfection . . . I never tasted anything of the fish kind half so exquisite . . . Besides subsisting the inhabitants . . . vast quantities are cured (not less than eight thousand barrels) every fall and sent down to the eastern states."

— Anna Jameson, *Winter Studies and Summer Rambles in Canada,* 1838.

Jesuit missionaries named the falls after the Virgin Mary in 1634. In winter, as it had the only running water for miles around, the area had become a gathering and fishing spot for the Indians and fur traders from the North West Company trading post, set up in 1783.

Two recipes for whitefish from *Culinary Landmarks,* Sault Ste. Marie, 1909.

WHITEFISH

Cover in a fish kettle, or tie up in a cloth, and suspend in boiling water to cover. Simmer 8-10 minutes per pound. After about 5 minutes, add a little vinegar or lemon juice. When cooked, drain carefully and serve garnished with parsley sprigs and accompanied with an egg sauce.

PLANKED WHITEFISH

Have a small piece of hardwood plank (soft wood leaves the taste of the wood). Prepare a piece of fish, brush it over with a little melted butter and olive oil. Lay it on the plank leaving a small space around the edges; cover this space with salt to prevent plank from burning. Bake in a quick oven (400°F). Brush off salt and serve on plank.

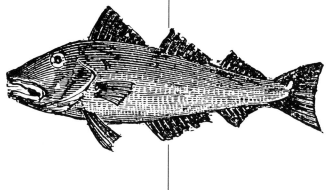

A view of Sault Ste. Marie and disembarking passengers from the steamer 'Collingwood,' June 16, 1899. The dock was at the foot of Pim Street, on St. Mary's Road.

The Northern Judge

In 1860, Colonel John Prince, whom we last heard of near Amherstburg, stepped off the steamer at Sault Ste. Marie. The little village of about 300 souls had recently been created district headquarters for the vast new judicial region of Algoma, and Prince had been appointed its first judge. At the time of his arrival, this one-time bustling community had shrunk to a shadow of its former self, its fur trade eclipsed, its locks destroyed in the war of 1812 and not yet rebuilt. Prince himself had practised law near Windsor, had pursued a brief military career remarkable for mercilessness during the 1837 rebellions, and had passed his last four years in Toronto as a member of the Legislative Council of Upper Canada. He was an enigmatic, morose personality, no longer young, one of the many lonely, misanthropic, hard-drinking bachelors who besprinkle the harsh pages of Ontario's early history. (In light of the first Prime Minister's and his own weaknesses it is amusing to find Prince writing at one point to urge John A. Macdonald "not to rely on cold water and tea and coffee alone, to sustain your not very robust and sometimes over-wrought frame and constitution in yr present arduous position!" Advice no doubt followed to the letter.) On arrival at this re-mote spot, Prince directed his steps to the boarding house of Mrs. Maria Hetherington who had been his landlady in Toronto, and who tucked him under her kindly and understanding wing. So much so that by the following summer he was writing proudly in his journal of the compliments lavished on his newly built house, and could add, "I give all the credit to Mrs. Hetherington in that respect because she deserves it, and the plan was hers and hers only." Accordingly (and with infinite logic), the planner, and her furniture, moved in, to look after him as his housekeeper for his remaining nine years. Prince never married Maria Hetherington, but for one of his irascible nature his references to her are always touchingly tender, docile and appreciative. One suspects not without reason. A typical entry in his diary, after presiding as Chairman of the General Quarter Sessions on June 11, 1867, runs, "Good Mrs. Hetherington came up and saw me home safely."

Prince died in 1870. His tombstone has been moved from one of the islands in Bellevue Park to the Sault Ste. Marie Museum. The Township of Prince is called after him.

Belle Vue Lodge, Judge John Prince's house, seen from the St. Marys River, Sault Ste. Marie.

Good Mrs. Hetherington's Cookbook

In March, 1861, Prince made a gift of a cookbook to Mrs. Hetherington. Inside its front cover she subsequently wrote her own cherished recipe for Chutney Sauce. It was plainly a favourite of the colonel's and a note from him precedes it:

"I believe that the annexed receipt is not to be found in any part of the world, except in <u>India</u>. <u>Mrs. Hetherington will not part with it</u>, but the making of the sauce from it may (and I think it would) realize a <u>nice living</u>. The stuff sold in Europe as 'Chutney Sauce' has nothing of the old <u>genuine</u> flavor or properties. J. P."

MRS. HETHERINGTON'S CELEBRATED INDIA "CHUTNEY SAUCE"*

[The celebrated sauce, every bit as fiery as the Judge himself!]

1 lb. salt
1 lb. mustard seed
1 lb. brown sugar
8 c. unripe gooseberries
12 oz. garlic
8 c. best vinegar
1 lb. raisins
6 oz. cayenne pepper.

Dry and bruise the mustard seed. Combine the sugar and some of the vinegar to make a syrup.

Dry the gooseberries and boil with half the vinegar. Bruise the garlic well in a mortar, and, with the remaining vinegar, thoroughly combine with all the ingredients. Tie this down close in sterile jars and in one month it will be fit to use, but will be better in 8 months — and <u>the longer it is kept the better</u>.

Gooseberries seem to have been quite common then, growing wild in Ontario. Try chopped underripe plums if you cannot obtain them.

ROSE HIP SAUCE FOR PUDDING

Remove seeds from rose hips. Soak them, boil till tender and pass through a sieve. Then stir in boiling wine till a thin cream, and sweeten to taste.

From *The Housekeeper's Encyclopedia* by Mrs. E. F. Haskell, New York, 1861, the book presented by Colonel Prince to Maria Hetherington.

The forests around Sault Ste. Marie afforded plentiful game.

Life With The Judge

The scene opposite notwithstanding, in a letter of 1868 to Prime Minister John A. Macdonald, Prince, then aged 72, grumbled, "I preferred this wild part of U.C. . . . because I was told (by some who knew better but were desirous of getting me hither) that Deer and other large Game were abundant; whereas I believe it to be the only part of North America where they do not exist!" He requested (fruitlessly) to be transferred to the North West Territory.

TO ROAST A NECK OR SHOULDER OF VENISON

[This and the recipe for turkey are from Mrs. Hetherington's cookbook.]

Roast without covering, 15 mins. to the lb. Baste with salted water and butter. Prepare a sauce with wine or jelly.

From John Prince's diary, 22 November 1867:
"A very cold morning and freezing hard. . . Shot 2 of our beautiful wild Turkey cocks. It cut my heart to do so, but I can't afford to keep them."

But about a month later more wild turkeys were roosting in his hen house, so perhaps he shot another in time for Christmas.

TO BAKE A TURKEY

Stuff with dressing seasoned with salt, pepper and summer-savory; sew up opening, truss and brush with butter. Have the oven a good but not raging heat; you should be able to count twenty while holding your hand in the oven. Baste bird every five minutes. Allow 2 to 2 1/2 hours for an average turkey. Serve with browned gravy, vegetables, and currant, grape or cranberry jelly.

"25 June 1861. Wrote to Mr. Walker [Hiram Walker was a distiller on the Detroit River, above Windsor] a long letter thanking him for the keg of Whisky he sent me last fall, and . . . Oats and Buckwheat and a barrel of Whisky which came the other [day] . . . ."

Thoughtful Mr. Walker! Still, whatever her thoughts on the whisky, the oats and buckwheat must have pleased Mrs. Hetherington who might have turned to the recipe for buckwheat cakes in her new cookbook.

RAISED BUCKWHEAT CAKES

Warm 4 c. water and stir in 1 T. molasses and 1 t. salt. Mix in enough buckwheat flour to make a batter, and stir in 1 T. brewer's yeast or 2 T. hop yeast. Let it rise. If it remains all night and becomes sour, add soda. Drop the batter by spoonfuls onto a hot griddle and fry. Serve as soon as baked.

September 3, 1886, Port Arthur. Sir John A. and Lady Macdonald look down from their railway car.

'A Horizontal View'

All eyes on the camera!

For a moment the small crowd gathered on the platform at Port Arthur (now Thunder Bay), is even more intrigued by the photographer than by the spectacle of Sir John A. Macdonald, first Prime Minister of the young Dominion of Canada, and Lady Macdonald. They were on the return leg of a 50-day, 6,000-mile, "ocean to ocean" journey which had given him a holiday, a knowledge of the great new country he was creating, and a chance to show himself to its new inhabitants.

It is a symbolic photograph — the infant transcontinental railway and the aging politician, whose grand vision it had been to bind the country together by its means. It had nearly killed him.

To one audience along his route, Macdonald typically made light of it. He told them he had scarcely dared hope he would live to travel along the finished railway. His friends [he said] had expected he might have to view it from the serene heights of heaven above. His enemies had supposed he would gaze up at it from the pit beneath.

"I have now disappointed both friends and foes" he continued gaily, "and am taking a horizontal view."

Here is a pudding from Bath, near Kingston, dedicated to the Old Chieftain himself.

SIR JOHN A. PUDDING

2 c. breadcrumbs
1 c. sugar
4 c. milk
4 eggs, separated
butter, size of an egg
grated rind of 1 lemon.

Beat the egg yolks well. Combine with breadcrumbs, milk, butter and lemon rind. Stiffly beat the egg whites. Sprinkle sugar over the top when done. Spread over the top of the pudding. Bake in oven a few minutes and serve with butter.

From *Dora's Cook Book* Bath, 1888.

A Railway construction crew working on a line north of the C.P.R.

The Great Railway

The most costly stretch of the wildly expensive railroad was east of Port Arthur. Here the work involved tunnelling through iron-hard rock and hewing ledges round cliffs towering hundreds of feet above the line. It cost more than $500,000 per mile, astronomical sums for the time. While bankers suffered breakdowns, 40,000 men and thousands of animals sweated, suffered, froze and, in some cases, died along the iron road itself. But it was completed in five years, half the time predicted. Small wonder that the railway captured the nation's imagination. The excitement penetrated even to the kitchens out of which came a spate of recipes for "Railroad Cake"!

RAILROAD CAKE (Miss Lillie Ross, Kingston.)

4 oz. butter
1 c. fine sugar
3 eggs
2 T. milk
1 t. vanilla *or* lemon
6 oz. plain flour
2 heaped t. baking powder
a little salt
icing sugar (optional).

Cream butter till white, then add sugar and beat well. Add eggs, beating in with 1 T. of the flour each; then milk and flavouring. Sift remaining ingredients together and combine well with mixture. Turn into a well buttered and floured sandwich tin. Bake in oven for 30–40 minutes. When cool, dust with icing sugar if wished.

Affairs prevented the Macdonalds from travelling on the first "ocean to ocean" C. P. R. train that left Montreal, June 28, 1886. However, Mrs. Arthur Spragge did travel on it and wrote a book about it. As she recounted, no sooner had she embarked than she discovered the Pullman she had entered, one of the Company's finest, was for men only. However, Mrs. Spragge delayed long enough to memorise every detail including the beautiful velvet upholstery, the seats and berths carved in cherry inlaid with brass, even (without a blush) the marble lavatories and bath "evidently much patronised between Montreal and Winnipeg." When a "very civil" black porter escorted her to her own place she found it "very common and ordinary" compared to the other. Later she witnessed the arrival of the Macdonalds' special train at Donald in the Rockies.

"Lady Macdonald [created] an immense sensation . . . by her occupancy of a well-cushioned seat immediately, above the cowcatcher; she . . . subsequently continued her journey to Port Moody [on it] . . . a feat which will doubtless become historical."

The Assiniboia heads down the Kaministiquia River. Behind the ships rise three wheat elevators, 1910.

Arthur In Thunderland

"Long before one reaches [Port Arthur and Fort William] one sees the mountainous wheat elevators in which much of the western harvest is stored until it can be shipped eastwards. They have been called the 'Castles of Commerce,' and from a distance they look like a combination of the great keep of a Norman fortress, with the pillars of Luxor built into it . . . . We made a very adventurous motor journey in the afternoon to see the lake among the mountains whence the water supply is obtained."

— Arthur Conan Doyle,
Our Second American Adventure, 1923.

Arthur Conan Doyle, creator of Sherlock Holmes, referred to Loch Lomond, a lake only seven miles southwest and 327 feet above the city's level. The waterworks was completed in 1909, yet fourteen years later, Conan Doyle commented that it was "so difficult of access that I was assured very few of the inhabitants had visited it." For years, construction of a water supply system from this source had been suggested, but the difficulties involved, including the excavation of a tunnel for nearly a mile through solid rock, had made it appear far beyond the means of the young and still small community of Fort William. In 1905, faced with 832 cases of typhoid (or nearly one in every six of the population) due to pollution of the Kaministiquia River from which its water then came, the little city somehow found the money. Three years later, on June 23, 1909, water from the newly completed Loch Lomond works started to flow into the city's mains and the typhoid problem was over.

"There, lying among virgin woods, the moose, the deer, the bear and the beaver, are common objects."

——Arthur Conan Doyle, describing the area of Loch Lomond, near Fort William, 1923.

GAME SOUP

[A simple version of a Scottish Highland game soup.]

Remains of any game
1 carrot
1 stick celery
1 turnip
1 onion, stuck with 2 cloves
sherry to taste.

Dice and reserve a few good pieces of game. Put remainder in pot. Add coarsely chopped carrot, celery and turnip, the whole onion, and stock to cover. Simmer 8 hours. Strain and skim. Add diced game and sherry and heat thoroughly.

From *The Blue Book,* produced by St. Paul's Anglican Church, Fort William, post 1908.

A society wedding, N. Algoma Street, Port Arthur, circa 1909. Margaret Smellie is at extreme right.

The Doctor's Girls

Dr. Thomas Smellie headed one of Thunder Bay's most distinguished families at the end of the last century and the first half of this. He was Medical Officer of Health until 1897, a difficult time of almost uncontrolled immigration into the little community. Later he was M. P. P. for Fort William during the traumatic years of the typhoid epidemic and the water supply problems. He fathered a family which included two redoubtable daughters, who grew up deeply imbued with their father's interests in health, medicine, and nutrition. Colonel Elizabeth Smellie, among many achievements, was mentioned in despatches in World War I and re-organized the Women's Canadian Army Auxiliary Corps during World War II. She was created a Commander of the British Empire, and received her LL.D. from the University of Western Ontario, the first ever awarded to a woman by that institution. Colonel Elizabeth's older sister, Margaret, was eclipsed by her remarkable sibling, but on the smaller stage of life in Thunder Bay, she was a woman of achievement. In 1918 she jointly compiled a war time cook book called *Recipes of War Time Dishes For The Housewife*. Two of its recipes are included below.

SOLDIER'S CAKE (no eggs)

1 lb. flour
1/2 lb. butter substitute
[butter will do in peace time!]
1 lb. raisins, chopped
1/4 lb. mixed peel
1 c. fresh or sour milk
1/2 lb. brown sugar
1 1/2 t. bicarb. of soda
1 1/2 t. mixed spice.

Finely chop mixed peel. Mix dry ingredients. Dissolve soda in 1 T. of milk, warmed. Stir into remaining milk and add to dry ingredients. Steam 2 hours in well greased and floured cake tin, then bake 1 hour in a slow oven.

SCOTCH POTATO SCONES*

[particularly good when fresh and hot]

2 c. fresh mashed potatoes
1 t. milk
3 T. melted butter
level t. salt
2/3 c. flour
1/4 t. baking soda.

Add soda to flour. To potatoes, work in milk, butter, salt, and flour to make a stiff dough. Roll out thinly. Cut in 6 inch circles. Brown well on gridiron on top of stove. Eat cold or hot with butter.

Red and white pine is loaded high on a flatcar, probably south east of Thunder Bay.

The Arrival of the Finns

Around 1900, the timber trade in Port Arthur was booming and skilled workers were in demand. In fact the Port Arthur Board of Trade, in an urgent appeal for lumber workers, expressed a preference for Finns and Scandinavians, with "experience in wood cutting and timber floating." The two Tenkula brothers from Finland, already in the country several years, responded to the demand. In 1901 the elder brother persuaded their younger sister, Eina, to come out and keep house for his big family. Before very long Eina had met a Finn Swede named Otto Wilan, and in 1906 married him. Otto, in fact, was not in the lumber business at all but a custom tailor, and numbered among his clients the city's elite: doctors, lawyers, bankers, magistrates. Just such figures as can be seen (in remarkably well-cut suits) in the wedding picture on the previous page, perhaps —who knows? -suited out for the occasion by Mr. Wilan himself!

The following recipes were donated by Eina's granddaughter, Kerine Budner, in the forefront of those concerned with conserving the traditions of the Finnish community in Thunder Bay, certainly one of the largest Finnish communities outside Finland. There is only room to print a few examples of their interesting cuisine. Several of the recipes came from Kerine's Finnish grandparents on both sides, all of whom arrived in Thunder Bay before 1903.

HEDELMAKEITTO (Cold fruit soup)

[Makes a delicious fruit compote. Serve it hot in winter, poured over the rice pudding (overleaf) if you wish, or cold in summer, with ice cream.]

$^1/_2$ lb. dried apples
$^1/_2$ lb. dried apricots
$^1/_2$ lb. prunes
$^1/_2$lb. raisins
1 t. cinnamon
1 c. sugar
2 qts water
2 T. potato flour or cornstarch.

Soak the apples for about an hour beforehand in a little water, to soften. Drain. Rinse other fruits. Combine all fruit with the sugar and cinnamon in a large pot. Cover with the 2 qts. water and simmer until fruit is tender. Don't overcook. Reduce heat to low; remove 1 c. liquid from pot. Mix flour or cornstarch with liquid until smooth. Return mixture to pot and simmer for a few minutes. Serve warm or cold. (Serves 8.)

Well wrapped small boys study curling form on the frozen Kaministiquia River.

Finnish Fare – A Northern Cuisine

According to Kerine Budner, this is heart-warming in winter, with either the cranberry sauce below, or the (hot) fruit soup on the previous page, ladled over it.

RIISI PUUROA

[Finnish rice pudding]

1 c. rice
4 c. milk
1 t. salt
3 t. sugar
$1/3$ t. cinnamon.

Wash rice. Bring milk to boiling point, add rice and stir as it boils. Constant stirring makes the rice creamy. When rice is soft, add salt, sugar and cinnamon. If stick cinnamon used, add it with the rice. (Can be eaten with milk or sugar alone. Also good with raisins, or blueberries.)

KLAPPA-PUUROA

[cranberry sauce]

[This recipe is from Kerine Budner's grandmother.]

Boil 1 c. cranberries and 1 c. sugar in 2 c. water till soft. Drain. Combine with $1/4$ c. cream of wheat.

LIVER LOAF

$1 \ 1/2$ lbs. liver
1 c. short-grain rice
1 t. brown sugar
2 eggs
$1 \ 1/2$ c. milk
2 large onions
pinch ginger or nutmeg
salt and black pepper.

Grind liver medium fine. Parboil rice for 10 minutes. Slightly beat eggs. Chop onions finely and fry till translucent. Fill an oiled casserole with the ingredients and bake in a 350°F oven for approximately 1 hour or until a knife comes out easily. The top turns quite brown. When done, cut into $1/2$ inch slices.

Indian women by Lake Makokibatan, on the Albany River.

A Meeting With Cecilia

I took a long journey north in the hope of finding authentic old Indian ways of preparing food. My destination was Lansdowne House, a village of 230 members of the Fort Hope Band of Ojibways, set in the vast inaccessible wilderness between the Manitoba border and James Bay. A little twin-engined plane took 2 hours to get there from Thunder Bay, via Fort Hope, a larger Ojibway community off the Albany River. By late May, the trees at Lansdowne House are barely in leaf and, off the dirt road, the half-thawed muskeg quakes underfoot. The village has a beautiful setting, spread over two islands, but is a sorrowful little place, refuse and empty oil drums lying about. Almost half of it is derelict, abandoned in the early 1980s by its Anglican parishioners after violent conflicts with some of the Catholic community.

The small Hudson Bay Company outlet has supplied the Indians for a very long time. Back in the eighteenth and early nineteenth centuries the northern fur trading posts successfully encouraged these Ojibways to come north from their hunting and fishing grounds on Lake Superior and adapt to a fur-trapping life-style, offering guns, kettles and supplies for furs. In winter the Band became nomadic, out on their traplines, but in summer they camped near the trading posts. This pattern remained more or less unchanged till the 1960s, when the building of government schools forced families to remain sedentary and obliged them to depend on welfare.

At Lansdowne House, the school with its friendly, curious children is the happiest place in the village, and here, between classes, Cecilia Sugarhead, teacher of Ojibway language and culture, talked about the old ways of preparing food, a few of which are still in use. Many of the foods traditionally associated with native cooking are unavailable this far north. There is no corn, wild rice or squash. Spruce tea is unfamiliar. There are two local teas.

MOUNTAIN ASH TEA.

A strong tea made from peeled mountain ash sticks, cut small and boiled.

CEDAR TEA

Much more effective for colds and headaches, Cecilia said, than the pills from the village's small clinic. Both needles and twigs are boiled in water.

As in the old days, to help the healing process Cecilia always throws an offering of a little tobacco onto the fire. ("An offering to whom?" I asked, to which she replied, shocked, "The Creator, of course.") Before the building of the school forced the Band to remain in the village for most of the year, her parents were constantly on the move. "When [they] left a place my mother would always throw an offering on the ground to give thanks." Cecilia said her father used to paddle to Sioux Lookout to purchase tobacco. It took him two to three months.

Preparing bannock

North of the Albany

BANNOCK

"Bannock was for travelling," said Cecilia. She suggested using 3 c. flour, 1 T. baking powder and water to mix. This is kneaded well and cooked with grease in a frying pan over a fire.

Regarding large game, Cecilia said she had never seen a deer in her life, but "there were caribou in the past." Her parents cooked the fur-bearing creatures which they trapped (otter, lynx, marten and mink), roasting or boiling them over a fire. She admitted that she didn't care for them. There were also geese, rabbits, and fish. Geese and rabbits were simply boiled. In the case of geese, dumplings were cooked in the stock. Rabbits were jointed, potatoes and carrots added and flour used to thicken the stock. Cecilia said that salt and pepper were unavailable when she was young.

When I showed Cecilia the picture on p.202 in which strips of sturgeon are drying on racks, she said she had seen sturgeon in the late 1980s. They had been quite common. Sturgeon or other fish oils, she said, were used as an alternative to moose grease, or, nowadays, to lard or oil, for frying. The fish is boiled and its thick fat rises to the top of the water. This is scooped off, washed, some of it made into soap and the rest kept for cooking and other purposes. Originally, before jars were available, it was stored in a large fish gut. She said that smoking the strips of fish kept the flies away. Drying the fish strips takes between 30 hours and two days, and is contingent on many variables of weather, wind and the smoking fire.

FISH FLAKE STEW

Use whitefish, suckers and other small fish. Broil them on a stick over a fire. Flake the cooked fish into a bowl. It is then stirred over low heat till brown and dry and this way does not go rotten. It used to be kept in birch bark containers to keep the flies off. When needed, add grease and blueberries.

Index of Recipes

Picture Credits